The Effective Entrepreneur

The Effective Entrepreneur

CHARLES B. SWAYNE

WILLIAM R. TUCKER

GENERAL LEARNING PRESS
250 James Street
Morristown, New Jersey 07960

PREFACE

The Great American Dream has traditionally held that the individual can achieve whatever position in society to which he aspires. For untold numbers, the road to success has been through the formation and management of a new business. Some motivations toward this activity include financial security, not only in the form of profits but also in the form of providing for one's children in later years, community respect as a leading citizen, opportunity to utilize one's talents, and the occasion to engage in the mainstream of American economic life.

One of the primary reasons for taming the American West was to satisfy these motivations. With the technological advancements of the 19th and 20th centuries, however, small businesses and entrepreneurial activity has suffered. Rapid transportation and communication, for example, have eliminated the small monopolies which once existed in small neighborhoods and rural communities. The economics of scale have gradually forced out many small businesses in favor of the larger ones. The resulting increased competition, higher start-up and development costs plus tremendously increased management sophistication, have resulted in the gradual decrease in the number of small businessmen and new successful businesses.

These developments have not gone unnoticed by economists, in and out of the federal government. Federally sponsored programs have evolved, designed to favor small businesses and the formation of new ones.

Small Business Investment Corporations (SBIC's) and the S.B.A. are only two examples. Similarly, venture capitalists seeking high potential profits have recognized the problems of the potential entrepreneur. These groups have established vigorous programs to seek out and finance potentially profitable new businesses.

With this rapid increase in the availability of financial resources to the entrepreneur, the failure rate of new businesses remains extremely high. This high failure rate demonstrates that more is involved in successful entrepreneurial activity than available capital, sound ideas, and hard work. The authors maintain that the missing factor is the entrepreneur and the way he manages his business.

The major thrust of this book deals with the nature of the environment with which the entrepreneur is forced to cope. The resulting management styles, policies, and procedures as well as the behavioral characteristics of successful entrepreneurs form the basic subject matter.

ACKNOWLEDGEMENTS

The authors wish to express their gratitude to the Board of Directors of The Entrepreneurial Assistance Group,[1] a venture capital firm specializing in providing capital for high-risk marketing concepts and outstanding entrepreneurs. These men — Gary Daymon, Dan Broughton, Bob McCready, Steve Frame, Jim Kreutzmann, Joe Smith, Allan Wilson, Frank Pritchard, Dick Didow, Roger Miller and Dennis Dean — have all had the opportunity to deal in depth with entrepreneurs. Most are entrepreneurs themselves; some have run their own businesses. All have a highly developed ability to evaluate people. In short, these experienced men have given the authors invaluable editorial comments and suggestions.

   Our thanks also go to Biff Bonnivier, Vice President of Marketing National Mobile Homes Division, National Mobile Homes, for his insights. Our special thanks go to E. M. Bevington, Executive Vice President of The Trane Company, whose entrepreneurial leadership inspired many of the concepts presented in this book. Ed Semb did the artwork and Helen Solberg labored over the many drafts of the manuscripts providing supurb administrative support. Errors and omissions are clearly our responsibility. It is our hope that those seriously concerned with entrepreneurial activity will submit their suggestions and comments.

Charles Swayne
William Tucker

---

[1] The Entrepreneurial Assistance Group, Inc. is a venture capital firm with representatives in Atlanta, Birmingham, Columbia, Indianapolis, Houston, Louisville, Milwaukee, New Orleans, Orlando, Richmond, and St. Louis. The headquarters is at 3326 Robinsdale, La Crosse, Wisconsin 54601.

FOREWORD

Capitalism, the economic system of the United States since the nation's inception, owes a considerable debt of gratitude to a small group of persons whose several functions have been termed entrepreneurial. Joseph Schumpeter, the economic theorist and defender of Capitalism, viewed the entrepreneur as the catalytic agent that made the economic system "go" and prosper. Peter Drucker, the management theorist concurred.

The role of the entrepreneur is not easily assumed however; Schumpeter, writing in 1942, in his classic *Capitalism, Socialism and Democracy*[1] spoke of the function and the rigors of the entrepreneur as follows:

> ... the function of entrepreneurs is to reform or revolutionize the pattern of production by exploiting an invention or, more generally, an untried technological possibility for producing a new commodity or producing an old one in a new way, by opening up a new source of supply of materials or a new outlet for products, by reorganizing an industry and so on.
>
> To undertake such new things is difficult ...
>
> To act with confidence beyond the range of familiar beacons and to overcome that resistance requires aptitudes that are present in only a small fraction of the population and that defines the entrepreneurial type as well as the entrepreneurial function. This function does not essentially consist in inventing anything or otherwise creating the conditions which the enterprise exploits. It consists in getting things done.

It seems to me that the task facing the would-be entrepreneur of today is even more awesome than the situation described by Schumpeter. The tremendous increase in regulatory bodies and in other organizations that concern themselves with both the "market" and "non-market" facets of the business firm have added complexity and frustration to the entrepreneur. The increase in and greater power of "adversary organizations" as well as the exceedingly rigorous competition in the world's market place by foreign business have also added to the difficulty of the task.

This book is an attempt to assist entrepreneurs and particularly the person who is seriously considering taking the big step. It is also aimed at the venture capitalist and college "Small Business Course" markets.

The authors of the book are a refreshing blend of academia and business. The businessman (Swayne) has previously authored a book which is being used on a number of college campuses as a graduate textbook.

The Effective Entrepreneur reflects the "two worlds" of the authors. Its early chapters are concerned with a study of the entrepreneur, his management style, and the behavioral characteristics of successful entrepreneurs. The authors have searched the literature on this score and the best contributions of entrepreneurial and management theorists are presented in conjunction with the authors' own contributions. Chapters Six and Seven of the book could have been called "Should you do" and "How to do it." The "Business Start-Up Model, Concept, Plan, and Implementation" is a most impressive work. Not only is the new entrepreneur alerted to the many pitfalls that face him and to the numerous things he must do and considerations he must engage in, but also the enormity of the task as depicted in Chapter Seven will undoubtedly dissuade some aspiring entrepreneurs from taking the step. With the high mortality rate that has attached itself to new business ventures, this might have beneficial consequences both for the individuals and for the economy.

Sherman Dallas
Professor of Industrial Management
Georgia Institute of Technology

CONTENTS

ILLUSTRATIONS

To those with capital: those willing to take high risks in order to obtain high rewards.

To entrepreneurs: may they always remember those who have invested in them and express their thanks by adhering to one overriding policy: *maximize the near term price of the voting common stock.*

1

INTRODUCTION —
SCOPE
AND
LIMITATIONS

During the past 50 years, authors have written a plethora of information dealing with the men who run organizations and the "how to" of running an organization. One need only look at the innumerable paperbacks on the current market dealing with the executive's life, his style, his politics, and his motivation. Likewise, a host of texts may be found dealing with every phase of a professional, mature organization: sales management, production management, personnel management, marketing management, ad infinitum. However, two important areas have either been largely overlooked or ignored by the authors of our generation.

1. *A study of the entrepreneur and his management style.* Some management authors have alluded to the vital and important role of the entrepreneur in the life cycle of organizations. For example, the authors of *Managers For Tomorrow* say, "It is the entrepreneur who stands at the creative beginning in this story of organizational life and death. The entrepreneur's peculiar delight is to create a business where none existed before and to do it usually in competition with well-established firms. The entrepreneur is so important in business that it seems strange that his vital role in our society is of such little concern to management theorists."[1]

2. *A study of how the entrepreneur should obtain his first sale.* The "how" is emphasized. There are a few works on what one should do to start up a business but the "how-to" has been left out.

This book is intended to bridge these gaps and was written with a threefold readership in mind.

A. For entrepreneurs and those who believe they are to become entrepreneurs, the book is designed to provide a framework, based on theoretical concepts, which allows one to evaluate his own characteristics, personality, behavior, and perspective to see if indeed he does fit the entrepreneurial profile. Chapter 7, "The Business Start-Up," is designed to provide a road map of the who, what, when, and how-to of starting up a business. One should be able to take this part and start up any business.

B. It is intended for venture capitalists, including not only those who run investment firms, but also franchisers and some of our largest American corporations. Some corporations have recently established their own separate venture capital organizations. General Electric has a department called New Business Development. Standard Oil of New Jersey has established Jersey Enterprises. "These corporations have goals beyond mere capital gains. They see their venture groups as a way to encourage development of new business which, if successful, may eventually become operating divisions of the parent corporation. With this in mind, the corporations are introducing a new wrinkle into their investment contracts — the provision that, if the venture becomes successful after a certain number of years, the corporation's venture capital group will have the opportunity to take over 100% of the total for a specified price. The entrepreneur gets what he is looking for, large capital gains, and the investing corporation acquires a prosperous new enterprise."[2]

When the venture capitalist decides whether or not to make an investment in a new organization, he probably takes four major constraints into consideration.

1. The Market

2. The Money Required

3. The Product or Service

4. The People Involved

This final factor, the people involved, is of more importance than the other three combined; but even more significant is the fact that 90% of the venture capitalists' decisions will be made on their evaluation of the man who will be in charge of the new business — The Entrepreneur — because *THE SINGLE MOST IMPORTANT VARIABLE IN THE SUCCESS OF ANY NEW VENTURE IS THE ENTREPRENEUR.*

This book will provide a ready benchmark for those with capital to help evaluate the man in whom they invest. Perhaps Lord Keynes inadvertently described the venture capitalist's dilemma in the simplest language when he noted that

> . . . newspaper competitors . . . have to pick out the six prettiest faces
> from a hundred photographs . . . each competitor (chooses) those which

he thinks likeliest to catch the fancy of other competitors, all of whom are looking at the problem from the same point of view.[3]

Thus, the venture capitalist and the franchisor, like the newspaperman, are trying to locate via evaluation those entrepreneurs — pretty faces — which he believes will win the contest — survive and become profitable. In short, this book provides a method of evaluating the men who are prospecting for the venture capitalist's funds. Chapter 7 is of benefit to those who actively participate in the startup of new businesses. Perhaps one of the best known of these men is Georges F. Doriot, a former Brigadier General in the U.S. Army and a Harvard Business School Professor. He steered the first publicly traded venture capital company — American Research and Development — from a few dollars in 1946 to $555,000,000 today. "Our aim is to build up creative men and their companies."[4] For franchisors, Chapter 7 is a must since any organization which assists in the startup of hundreds of businesses, which franchisors do, needs a practical framework in order to get the business off to a fast start.

C. As a supplement to those colleges and universities who are placing greater emphasis on small-business management, some potential applications of the text include the following:

1. It is designed to serve as a supplemental reading for students at all levels who are contemplating starting a new business or consulting in this area.

2. It can be used as a supplemental text in advanced accounting and finance courses from which many students enter the business consulting field.

3. It is designed to be used as a text in those courses dealing with venture capital.

4. It could be used as the basis for a capstone course in small-business management.

5. It could be used as a supplement to courses discussing small-business administration loans.

6. It could be used as a text in minority business courses.

These pages are intended to allow a comparison between the academic view toward business and the actual world of an entrepreneur. This will help the student bridge the gap from theory to practice.

In writing this book, the authors realized at the beginning that little established theory existed as a guide. While popular magazines have traditionally taken delight in writing success stories in the Horatio Alger tradition, no thread of continuity exists. As in all new fields of this type, the first step towards understanding the seemingly complex is to report and interpret empirical observations. That is the task we have set out to accomplish.

The scope, limitations, and design of this book are as follows:

1. *The Effective Entrepreneur* is concerned only with entrepreneurs. Entrepreneurs are defined as those individuals who *successfully* conceive of new business ventures, organize and start them and manage them through their initial struggle for survival. The word successfully is in italics. This book deals only with observations of successful entrepreneurs. Hereafter, the reader should mentally add the word "successful" when the word "entrepreneur" is used.

2. *The Effective Entrepreneur* is based upon the authors' undocumented observations of hundreds of entrepreneurs for whom they have consulted and observed firsthand. Entrepreneurial behavorial characteristics are described which, the authors feel, offer the greatest explanatory power of success. Of necessity, the central tendency of the various behavioral characteristics are described for the observed population of entrepreneurs.

The reader is cautioned against trying to apply every characteristic, described herein, in any situation. Very few have or ever will possess them all. Some possess few if any. In Figure 1 the reader will see that the dark portion — This Book — is geometrically small relative to the set of successful entrepreneurs. Most entrepreneurs, however, have a large number of these described behavioral characteristics.

Another area warrants caution by the reader. It stems from the fact that the book is based only on successful entrepreneurs. Unsuccessful entrepreneurs and non-entrepreneurs may

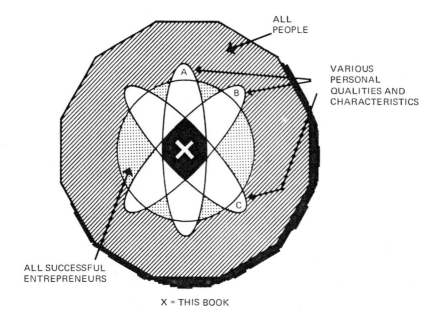

FIGURE 1. Set of Qualities Versus "This Book."

possess some and, even in a few cases, many of the described behavioral characteristics. The important point is that the individual having many of these characteristics is not guaranteed success. He does, however, have an increased probability of success.

As discussed in Item 6, which follows, little meaningful research has been conducted concerning the entrepreneur. Much of the framework of the model presented is based on theoretical models designed for explaining the behavior and performance of managers of large well-established businesses. Because of the nature of the differences between entrepreneurial management and professional management, the applicability of these models may be questioned. In other words, maybe different approaches or the inclusion of different characteristics would offer greater explanatory power. Only meaningful research will resolve this question. From this vantage point, however, the authors feel that the model presented is the best available.

3. *The Effective Entrepreneur,* being based upon observation, is best described as a positive, not a normative model.

That is, the entrepreneur and his world are described "as they are," not the way they should be.

The reader is once again cautioned in applying the results of this book. The real world is continually changing. Since the book is based on contemporary America, it obviously has very limited application outside this area. Similarly, even changes in the American scene must be considered in applying the results of *The Effective Entrepreneur*.

A second point must be considered in the application of a positive model. Simply because "this is the way it is" should not be construed to mean that "this is the way it should be." As pointed out in appropriate places throughout the book, practitioners as well as researchers may take exception to what is reported. At critical points, conflicting arguments are presented to allow the reader to make up his own mind.

One of the critical characteristics of an entrepreneur is an innovative nature. The reader is urged to be innovative in the interpretations and application of this work.

4. *The Effective Entrepreneur* is primarily concerned with "first-time" entrepreneurs — that is, those who have not yet made it really big. Once an entrepreneur has made his first quantum jump, his values, personality and behavior are slightly altered. Although this shift is briefly discussed in the book, one should keep in mind that the focus of this book is on the "first-time" entrepreneur.

5. *The Effective Entrepreneur* is designed to be as general in scope as possible. It is not restricted to any particular industry or type of business, such as service, manufacturing, or retailing. While technical expertise in a particular industry or business is necessary for the entrepreneur, it is assumed that he has acquired it through personal education or by surrounding himself with those who possess the necessary expertise. This book is concerned only with the entrepreneur — his psychological characteristics and the way he manages.

6. *The Effective Entrepreneur* can be viewed as both an appeal and challenge to those interested in entrepreneurial activity. The authors, and hopefully the readers, are aware of

the limitations of a study such as this. Personal observation cannot replace hard data based on sound research design. The scarcity of meaningful research by economists, psychologists, and management researchers, however, has been the impetus for this book.

An appeal is made to venture capitalists, franchisors, entrepreneurs, management consultants and other readers who, as well as the authors, are interested in entrepreneurial activity. Critical comments, suggestions, and personal observation are requested to improve subsequent editions of this book.

A challenge is issued to economists, psychologists, and management researchers to join with the authors and conduct meaningful research into entrepreneurial activity and the entrepreneur. The potential benefits to society are tremendous. These benefits include a greater understanding of the dynamic growth aspects of our economy, reduction of the economic waste and personal trauma associated with the failure of new businesses, and more meaningful involvement and more rapid integration of our minorities into the mainstream of American life.

SUMMARY

In summary, the authors maintain that the environment the entrepreneur faces requires him to be significantly different from professional managers. These differences are reflected in certain behavioral characteristics, management styles, philosophies, and methods. Since most research and writing about business managers has been aimed toward managers of mature and stable organizations, entrepreneurial management is a relatively neglected area of investigation.

It is the purpose of this book to elucidate those behavioral characteristics, styles, philosophies, and methods associated with successful entrepreneurial management. Chapters 2 through 6 deal with these items. Chapter 7 presents a road map to be used by potential entrepreneurs, which covers the important steps in a business startup. Chapter 8 summarizes the book and then looks at the forces and expected changes that will occur in entrepreneurial activity over the immediate future.

NOTES

[1] Rohrer, Hibler, and Replogle, *Managers For Tomorrow*, New American Library, 1969, page 259.

[2] University of Toronto, School of Business, Tapes "Seminar on Venture Capital," Time, Inc., 1972.

[3] John Keynes, *The General Theory of Employment Interest and Money*, Harcourt, Brace & Co., 1936, page 156.

[4] "A Risk Capitalist Bids a Golden Adieu," *Business Week*, January 22, 1972, page 85.

2

**BUSINESS
LIFE
CYCLE**

In the previous chapter the point was made that the entrepreneurial environment is of a unique nature. This unique nature, in turn, requires specialized behavioral characteristics and management philosophies. It is the purpose of this chapter to spell out in greater detail the underlying reasons for the uniqueness of the entrepreneurial environment and the nature of entrepreneurial management.

Economists have developed models that describe the so-called life cycle of a business. The life cycle of a business can be compared to the life cycle of man; that is, businesses tend to develop through four stages.

1. Birth and struggle for survival

2. A period of rapid growth or adolescence

3. A vigorous stage of prolonged maturity

4. Senescence, with its decline, decay and eventual death[1]

In managerial terms these four developmental stages in organizations may be called:

1. Entrepreneurial Management

2. Personal Management

3. Professional Management

4. Obsolescent Management

Figure 2 represents the type of management that prevails during the life of a business. *The time axis along the bottom is not only a function of how well the business shifts its management emphasis, but also it is a function of the growth rate of the industry.*[2]

ENTREPRENEURIAL MANAGEMENT

The start-up or birth stage of a new business is best characterized as one of a high degree of uncertainty. The major goal of the entrepreneur is to develop a profitable base to insure survival. To generate

13

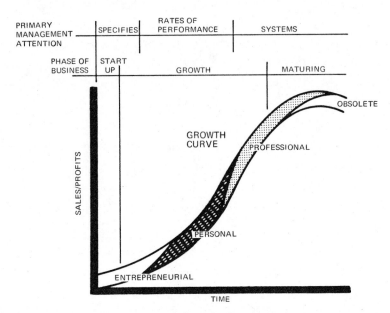

FIGURE 2. Growth Curve

these necessary profits, sales and production must be developed along with the control of costs.

The effect of uncertainty on the attainment of these goals and on the characteristics of entrepreneurial management determines the difference between entrepreneurs and non-entrepreneurs.

Of necessity, the development of a reliable sales base is of prime concern. Regardless of the degree of planning involved prior to start-up, the new business faces a tremendous challenge: the establishment of a known business name, acceptance of product or service by customers, and creation of a nucleus of stable customers to name but a few. A counter-reaction by competitors can also be added to the list.

If production is part of the new business, quality control, product design, and efficient operation of the equipment become critical to the entrepreneur. This list could be endless. It must include suppliers, new employees, government, credit sources, and many others. The important point is that no previous guidelines or experience exists.

In every case, the lack of previous experience, and a non-existent or very small operating base, force this uncertainty on the entrepreneur.

How does it affect his management? *Of necessity he must become concerned with the specifics of his business. He will try to digest all information available about his business and make all decisions. His management style may be described as neither well-planned nor controlled. "It is more impulsive than cautious. It is apt to be flexible, erratic, and utterly dependent upon immediate resourcefulness. It knows few systems or procedures. Lines of authority and responsibility expand and contract, shift and waver around individual managers . . . adaptability, flexibility, and opportunism are the organization's key to survival . . . the organization depends on the drive and resourcefulness of one man . . . (the entrepreneur) seldom delegates well. He seldom uses sophisticated systems and refined methods of control."[3] The management acts as the customers react. Emphasis is on selling and the primary reward to management is in terms of stock ownership.*

Once the business gets off the ground, larger production runs require knowledge about the efficiencies of manufacturing. Due to the increased number of employees communication cannot exist through the present informal organization. Quite often additional capital must be secured and new financial controls are needed. Thus, the entrepreneur finds himself burdened with unwanted management responsibilities. At this point in time a leadership crisis occurs.[4]

PERSONAL MANAGEMENT

Having survived the entrepreneurial stage, the dominant characteristic of the personal-management stage is growth. Management no longer must be obsessed with developing a base or foundation. Management energy is now directed toward extracting the maximum benefit from its competitive advantage. During this period, rates of performance become critical measures of performance.

This phase of management is characterized by a centralized and functional organizational structure, a top-management style that is directive, a control system that is largely dependent upon loose standards and cost centers, and a shifting of management reward emphasis towards salary and merit increases. The manager and his key supervisors take most of the responsibility for instituting direction, while lower-level supervisors are treated more as functional specialists than as autonomous decision makers.

Although the directive techniques channel employee energy more efficiently into growth, they eventually become inappropriate for controlling a larger, more diverse and complex organization. Lower-level employees find themselves restricted by an ever-increasing cumbersome and centralized hierarchy. They have come to possess more direct knowledge about markets and machinery than do leaders at the top; consequently, they feel torn between following procedures and taking initiative on their own.[5]

This period of youth in the organizational cycle is characterized by an informal style of management. The founder will usually have surrounded himself with a competent team that is capable of survival. The organization is run in an informal, intuitive way. Specialization, formal systems, explicit procedures, policies and communication structures are lacking until the last few months of this phase.

PROFESSIONAL MANAGEMENT

Most of the management literature available today concerns this phase of management development. It would be redundant to devote attention to it here. Suffice to say that professional management involves profit maximization, lower profit margins, and longer time horizons. Organization, control systems, and sophisticated planning techniques are some of the burning issues faced by professional managers in mature organizations.

OBSOLESCENT MANAGEMENT

The man in charge no longer keeps up with new developments: the market has shifted; its products and services have become antiquated, and more importantly, the people in the organization have lost their zip. The organization is doomed.

The obvious conclusion to be drawn from the preceding section is that *the primary attention of the manager and his perspective on his business changes as his business progresses through the various stages of development.* The entrepreneur is concerned with specifics and views his business as an extension of himself. The professional manager, on the other hand, is concerned with the integration of systems and the long-range planning necessary for long-term growth.

With the changing demands placed upon the manager as the business goes from infancy to maturity, the question must be asked "Can one man do it all?" Is entrepreneurial management sufficently different from professional management that different men are required? The answer in most cases is yes! *The majority of entrepre-*

*neurs begin to lose effectiveness long before the organization ap-
proaches maximum size and maturity.*

The management consulting firm of Rohrer, Hibler and Replogle
has investigated this problem. They have catalogued the most common symptoms that have enabled firms and managements to make
this transition from infancy to maturity.[6]

1. *From Large to Small Profit Margins.* Many business enterprises owe their existence to the fact that competition at the
time of their origin was not of the cutthroat variety. However, businesses seldom labor long in virgin territory; the
superior methodology of today becomes commonplace tomorrow. When a company is riding ahead of the pack, it is
easy to become accustomed to wide profit margins; in fact,
it may take its success for granted. Its management may turn
a deaf ear toward those who would counsel them to plan for
the future, rather than to wait for competition to catch up.
Those companies that make the transition do so by coming
up with more original ideas, by improving methods, by add-
ing capable manpower, and by cutting costs.

2. *From Random Growth to Planned Growth.* As sales increase, personnel are added and machinery and equipment
are purchased. New departments come into being, not because their need has been foreseen, but because there seems
to be no other way of solving the problems brought on by
increased size. Then as competition becomes keener, it is
more apparent that future sales are to be based on the ability
to anticipate the customer needs of tomorrow and not
solely on the ability to fill the orders of today. Planned
growth replaces random growth and the consequent im-
balance throughout the plant.

3. *From Laissez-faire to Systematic Manager Development.*
How often have we heard it said: "All the new executive
needs to know is where his desk is, who his secretary is, and
it is up to him to find out what his new assignment is all
about!"? Many companies still cling to this idea, and so let
their executives spin their wheels before making any forward
progress. After all, training in the techniques of management
can be as specific as the training prescribed in any other field.

The company that lets manager development happen instead of making it happen is inviting one of the most critical blocks to organizational growth.

4. *From Impulsive Management to Objective Management Controls.* In the entrepreneurial stage, the manager reacts to the needs of the moment, relying on his own ingenuity to come up with the right answers. He also deals directly with all members of the organization, not just the department heads. The manager of the more mature company operates through controls. He knows where he makes money and where he loses it and can tell at a glance what effect is caused by any changes he has initiated through his directives.

5. *From One Product to a Diverse Enterprise.* The entrepreneurial spirit and the products that made the founder successful cannot be relied on forever. There must be a wellspring of spirit that flows into new products and new markets so that the company can keep growing. These are the facts. If the organization does not provide a creative, entrepreneurial climate in which new product ideas can germinate, it is bound to succumb sooner or later to hardening of the markets.

All of the above five symptoms of loss of entrepreneurial effectiveness point to a leadership crisis. New accounting and financial controls are needed. Perhaps additional capital must be secured. Employees who are added may not share the excitement that was there when the organization was smaller and informal. The informal communication itself becomes a hindrance as opposed to an asset. The question the organization must answer at this point is "Who is to lead a company out of confusion and solve the managerial problems confronting it?"[7] "Quite obviously, a strong manager is needed who has the necessary knowledge and skill to introduce new business techniques. But this is easier said than done. *The entrepreneur often hates to step aside even though he is probably tempermentally unsuited to be a manager.*"[8]

Examination of Figure 3 illustrates this concept. *The man most effective in getting an organization off to a fast start is the man who is least effective in other phases of organizational development.*[9] The first phase of the business demands attention to specifics. The entrepreneur who possesses the ability to delegate (curves ED and ER) will accomplish the job, but not nearly as effectively and quick-

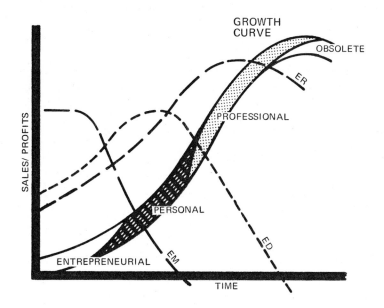

ER–EFFECTIVENESS OF THAT
    VERY RARE ENTREPRENEUR
    WHO DELEGATES AND CAN
    "MANAGE" IN THE TRADITIONAL
    SENSE

ED–EFFECTIVENESS OF THOSE
    ENTREPRENEURS WHO
    CAN DELEGATE

EM–EFFECTIVENESS OF MOST
    ENTREPRENEURS

FIGURE 3. Entrepreneurial Effectiveness Versus Growth

ly as the man who must do everything himself. With the various
specifics (Chapter 7 of the book gives an insight into the specifics
involved) that must be accomplished, we need a centralized decision-
maker and doer; not just a man who is a project leader.

Most entrepreneurs cannot delegate, hence the loss of effectiveness as the business grows due to the required reliance on middle
management. The man must be mature enough and flexible enough
to shift his *state of mind* from an entrepreneur to a personal manager
and then to a professional manager. If the man cannot make the
mental shifting of gears, he must remove himself from active leadership, else his business will die. He has no alternative.

Tex Thorton, the founder of Litton Industries, conveys the dilemma of becoming big. "You wonder why we don't have more multi-billion dollar companies around. There are so many that start with promise, but what happens? I think it's because one, two, or three men build a company to the extent of their capacity and don't let go. They feel insecure if they don't make all the decisions. Yet the company's growth has saturated their capabilities. Three times I've started small, and as the companies grew, I've had to discipline myself to decentralize. It wasn't easy the first time, but you've got to do it or you can't grow."[10]

The next important concept demonstrated in Figure 3 is that he who can both delegate and adapt to professional management techniques obtains a higher degree of effectiveness than the other types of entrepreneurs illustrated. Although initially not as effective as most entrepreneurs, this man, by nature of his versatility, his intimate knowledge of the history of the organization and its industry, and his almost irreplaceable understanding of the present state of affairs of the business, reaches the peak of his value to the organization after most entrepreneurs have outlived their usefulness. An "all things to all people" man is so rare that we will not dwell on him. Likewise the entrepreneur who learns to delegate is so relatively rare that we will not devote a great deal of time to him. It is fair to state that a new kind of entrepreneur is emerging. He can delegate. He is a product of our current society, albeit not one in overabundance. Suffice to say that *the main difference between the entrepreneur who builds a giant or a series of giants is his delegating ability and his adaptibility to sophisticated management.*

There are not many men who have shifted from entrepreneurial to personal to professional management successfully, but those who have will agree that during their entrepreneurial stage their *state of mind* was that of an entrepreneur. He played the part, albeit for only a while, of the man we will mentally dissect.

SUMMARY

In summary, the development of a business and the resultant management styles can be compared with the life cycle of man. The entrepreneur stage is filled with a high degree of uncertainty. The primary source of uncertainty being survival, the entrepreneur must develop styles and methods that are highly flexible and responsive.

Once the firm becomes established, it enters a rapid growth stage and then progresses into an adult or mature stage. As this development occurs, management must change its emphasis from survival to the coordination of complex and interrelated systems for maximum performance.

A critical question is whether an entrepreneur can change his style as his business matures. Evidence exists to support the point that very few can. The primary reason can be traced to the entrepreneur's inability to delegate authority during maturation. This evidence also supports the contention of the authors that entrepreneurs differ from professional managers and warrant special study.

Chapter three looks at the entrepreneur from a different vantage point. The major emphasis is on those factors that motivate the entrepreneur to assume the degree of uncertainty associated with starting a new business.

NOTES

[1] Rohrer, Hibler, and Replogle, *Managers For Tomorrow*, New American Library, 1969, page 258.

[2] Larry E. Greiner, "Evolution and Revolution as Organizations Grow," *Harvard Business Review*, July–August, 1972, page 39.

[3] Rohrer, Hibler, and Replogle, *op. cit.*, page 260.

[4] Larry E. Greiner, *op. cit.*, page 39.

[5] Larry E. Greiner, *op. cit.*, page 41.

[6] Rohrer, Hibler, and Replogle, *op. cit.*, page 266.

[7] Larry E. Greiner, *op. cit.*, page 42.

[8] *Ibid.*

[9] See for example J. R. Harris. "Factors Affecting the Supply of Industrial Entrepreneurship in Nigeria", mimeographed paper read at the Yale Growth Seminar, December 1966.

[10] "The Entrepreneur Luck and Pluck," *Forbes*, September 15, 1967, page 201.

3

ENTREPRENEURIAL
MAKEUP

Trade journals, newspapers, and popular magazines frequently cite stories of people who, in one way or another, have successfully started a business and made it blossom into a beautiful rose. The implication is that the only requirement is a good idea and a little capital and one is sure to succeed, make basketfuls of money, and lead a very enjoyable and enriching life.

Research into the statistics of business failures, however, reveals that about 72% of businesses started fail in their first two years. Of equal importance is the increase in the number of firms engaged in business consulting, franchising organizations, and firms involved in buying patentable ideas. All these statistics point to one very important point: an idea and a little money do not insure a successful entrepreneur.

Reasons cited for failure are many. They include such things as lack of capital, market depression, poor location, ad infinitum. The authors and others have found, however, that one of the necessary ingredients for successful entrepreneurship is a unique or different set of personality characteristics. It becomes of utmost importance to identify those personality characteristics that go into making the entrepreneur. Few people can enjoy the life style of an entrepreneur. "There's just not enough money in the world to compensate anybody to go through what an entrepreneur goes through in building a company. It's a terrible experience."[1] While it is realized that different entrepreneurial situations require varying personality characteristics, a basic understanding is still needed of the men who desire, need, and require the excitement and frustrations of starting up a new business.

SWAYNE

Entrepreneurs must possess at least two very strong personality traits — ego drive and empathy.[2]

Let us define exactly what we mean by ego drive and empathy. *Ego drive is an inner desire and need that makes an individual feel that he just must succeed.* This desire will vary from individual to individual, depending on his need for self-esteem. This need for self-esteem by the entrepreneur will be further discussed in the next section concerning Maslow's hierarchy of needs.

The marketplace provides a powerful means of enhancing his ego. "His self-picture improves dramatically by virtue of conquest."[3]

Empathy is the people interaction ability to understand how another feels without necessarily becoming sympathetic. The degree to which an individual can perceive and read another's inner feelings is largely due to the amount of attention, love, freedom, and interaction that he received with his parents during his childhood. In general, the greater the child-parent interaction, the greater the empathic ability.

The man with good empathy senses the reactions of others and is able to adjust to these reactions. He is not bound by one single way of getting things done, but moves in terms of real interaction between himself and others.

The entrepreneur must possess both empathy and ego drive not only in intensity but also in a certain balance. *Intensity is a must.* His innerself MAKES him succeed and allows him to succeed by understanding others. The balance between the two may vary from entrepreneurial situation to situation but will fall within a certain range.

Strong ego drive, strong empathy — An entrepreneur who has a great deal of both empathy and strong inner drive will be at or near the top in the marketplace.

Weak ego drive, strong empathy — A man with fine empathy but too little drive may be a splendid person but will be unable to deal effectively. This is the "nice guy." Everyone likes him, and from all appearances he should turn out to be one of the best men. He somehow "doesn't make it." People end up liking him, but buying from the company down the street. He will get along with people, but he does not have the inner hunger to move his people that final one foot. It is the last element of the conquest which empathy alone cannot achieve and where the assertive quality of ego drive becomes the all-important essential.

Strong ego drive, weak empathy — A man with much drive but too little empathy will bulldoze his way through to some successes but he will miss a great many and will hurt his business through his lack of understanding of people.

Weak ego drive, weak empathy — A man without much empathy or drive should not actually be in a managerial position, much less in an entrepreneurial role.

Note in Figure 4 the distribution of 100 entrepreneurs. Again, INTENSITY is a must; the balance will vary slightly with the situation. One should study Figure 4 before continuing, as a thorough understanding of this illustration is essential.

Since the entrepreneur's business is in a "fight for life" situation,

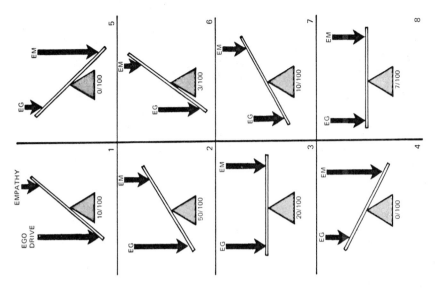

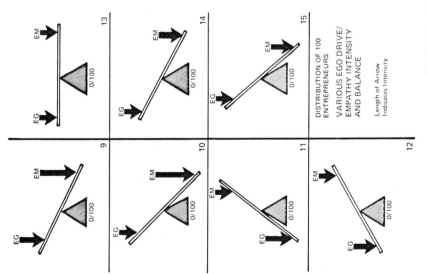

FIGURE 4. Entrepreneurial Ego Drive/Empathy Balance and Intensity.

his ego drive may need to be stronger than his empathy. The man with too much empathy, the "nice guy," does not have the proper mental balance to take the often immediate and swift action required, especially if that action involved the firing of people. Equipped with a strong empathy and an extremely strong ego drive, the entrepreneur is prepared to fight the business battle for survival.

Many distinguished authors of management theory have written in the area of this inner need or ego drive to succeed or to conquer. The following is a brief summary of the writings of some of the more important authors.

SCHUMPTER

Schumpter states that entrepreneurs are *driven by will for power* but they are slightly ahead of their time, that *they get things done through sheer energy and will power, that they do not worry about social constraints*, and that they are present in all ethnic groups.

McCLELLAND

McClelland stresses the influence of parents on the entrepreneur. Parents who constantly instill high standards that can be and are achieved, but do not interfere with a child's achievement and share emotionally (but not overemotionally) with the achievement will produce entrepreneurs. These parents instill the standards for excellence because of their religious world view, the father's profession, and the parents' position as head of the family. This type of upbringing breeds a high need for achievement and manifests itself in the form of *one who desires situations that require skill, a desire to take responsibility for an action, and a need to have a quantifiable yardstick for measuring task performance.*

McClelland's research led him to the conclusion that the need for achievement was a major motivating force. This n-Achievement is defined as the desire to do well, not so much for the sake of social recognition or prestige, but for the sake of an inner feeling of personal accomplishment.

HAGEN

Hagen says that the entrepreneurial personality takes many generations to develop. The generations go through the following stages. The first is the traditional authoritarian child-rearing stage which produces a non-innovative child. Then, if there is a "status withdrawal," (status withdrawal can be produced by a forced change in a family environment, a loss of respect on the part of society for previously valued symbols, anachronistic status symbols, or a rejection of expected status) something unusual happens. Status withdrawal produces anger and anxiety which, in turn, produce a suppression of values and an introversion and isolationism. Against this background there emerges a rejection of the husband on the part of the mother coupled with an over-protection of the child. This produces a child who possesses a high need for order, economy, and achievement. As the child matures, the society around him attempts to block his advancement. This social blockage produces eventual entrepreneurial behavior — *one who is a creative problem solver, who has a high need for achievement, and who has an air of order and autonomy.*

MASLOW

Over the past few years, we have witnessed many different attempts to understand and account for human behavior. Maslow, in 1954, put forth his views concerning a man's needs.[4] His work was directed toward those within an organization and an attempt to help management understand their workers. Basically, he views man's needs in a hierarchical form. Before one is motivated by a "higher" need, the "lower" needs must be at least partially satisfied. The late Professor Douglas McGregor[5] of the Massachusetts Institute of Technology has condensed Maslow's theory. Below is a restatement of Professor McGregor's work.

Physiological Needs

> Man is a wanting animal — as soon as one of his needs is satisfied, another appears in its place. This process is unending. It continues

from birth to death. Man continuously puts forth effort — works, if you please — to satisfy his needs. More specifically, all behavior can be traced to a man's desire to gain or maintain.

Human needs are organized in a series of levels — a hierarchy of importance. At the lowest level, but preeminent in importance when they are thwarted, are his physiological needs. Man lives by bread alone, when there is no bread. Unless the circumstances are unusual, his needs for love, for status, and for recognition are inoperative when his stomach has been empty for a while. But when he eats regularly and adequately, hunger ceases to be an important need. The sated man has hunger only in the sense that a full bottle has emptiness. The same is true of the other physiological needs of man — for rest, exercise, shelter, protection from the elements.

A satisfied need is not a motivator of behavior! This is a fact which is . . . ignored in the conventional approach to the management of people. An example will make the point. Consider your own need for air. Except as you are deprived of it, it has no appreciable motivating effect upon your behavior.

Safety Needs

When the physiological needs are reasonably satisfied, needs at the next higher level begin to dominate man's behavior — to motivate him. These are the safety needs for protection against danger, threat, and deprivation. Some people mistakenly refer to these as needs for security. However, unless man is in a dependent relationship where he fears arbitrary deprivation, he does not demand security. The need is for the "fairest possible break." When he is confident of this, he is more than willing to take risks. But when he feels threatened or dependent, his greatest need is for protection, for security.

The fact needs little emphasis that since every industrial employee is in at least a partially dependent relationship, safety needs may assume considerable importance. Arbitrary management actions, behavior which arouses uncertainty with respect to continued employment or which reflects favoritism or discrimination, and unpredictable administration of policy — these can be powerful motivators of the safety needs in the employment relationship at every level, from worker to vice president. In addition, the safety needs of managers are often aroused by their dependence downward or laterally. This is a major reason for emphasis on management prerogatives and clear assignments of authority.

Social Needs

When man's physiological needs are basically (not necessarily totally) satisfied and he is no longer fearful about his physical welfare, his social needs become important motivators of his behavior. These are such needs as those for belonging, for association, for acceptance by one's fellows, and for giving and receiving friendship and love.

Management knows today of the existence of these needs, but it is often assumed quite wrongly that they represent a threat to the organization. Many studies have demonstrated that the tightly knit, cohesive work group may, under proper conditions, be far more effective than an equal number of separate individuals in achieving organizational goals. Yet management, fearing group hostility to its own objectives, often goes to considerable lengths to control and direct human efforts in ways that are inimical to the natural "groupiness" of human beings. When man's social needs — and perhaps his safety needs, too, — are thus thwarted, he behaves in ways which tend to defeat organizational objectives. He becomes resistant, antagonistic, and uncooperative. But this behavior is a consequence, not a cause.

Ego Needs

Above the social needs — in the sense that they do not become motivators until lower needs are reasonably satisfied — are the needs of greater significance to management and to man himself. They are the egoistic needs, and they are of two kinds:

1. Those needs that relate to one's self-esteem: needs for self-respect and self-confidence, for autonomy, for achievement, for competence, and for knowledge.

2. Those needs that relate to one's reputation: needs for status, for recognition, for appreciation, and for the deserved respect of one's fellows.

Unlike the lower needs, these are rarely satisfied; man seeks indefinitely for more satisfaction of these needs once they have become important to him. However, they do not usually appear in any significant way until physiological, safety, and social needs are reasonably satisfied. Exceptions to this generalization are to be observed, particularly under circumstances where, in addition to severe deprivation of physiological needs, human dignity is trampled upon. Political revolutions often grow out of thwarted social and ego, as well as physiological needs.

The typical industrial organization offers only limited opportunities for the satisfaction of egoistic needs to people at lower levels in the hierarchy. The conventional methods of organizing work, particularly in mass-production industries, give little heed to these aspects of human motivation. If the practices of "scientific management" were deliberately calculated to thwart these needs — which, of course, they are not — they could hardly accomplish this purpose better than they do.

Self-Fulfillment Needs

Finally — a capstone, as it were, on the hierarchy — there are the needs for self-fulfillment or self-actualization. These are the needs for realizing one's own potentialities, for continued self-development, for being creative in the broadest sense of that term.

The conditions of modern industrial life give only limited opportunity for these relatively dormant human needs to find expression. The deprivation most people experience with respect to other lower-level needs diverts their energies into the struggle to satisfy *those* needs, and the needs for self-fulfillment remain below the level of consciousness.

Figure 5 presents an oversimplification of Maslow's need hierarchy. Only as one level of the hierarchy is partially filled or satisfied does the next level serve as a motivator. For the manager of an organization to motivate his employees most effectively, he must determine where in the hierarchy the individual falls. The manager can then motivate the employee by using appropriate tools designed to help fill an existing level or by appealing to the next highest level.

The shaded portions of Figure 6 demonstrate that *before a next-higher level can serve as a motivator, the existing level or lower level must be filled or nearly filled.* Figure 6 also shows where many people find themselves in today's technological society.

But what about the entrepreneur? Is he significantly different? He is! Figure 7 depicts how the entrepreneur's need-level fulfillment is distributed. Note *the extreme need for self-esteem and the relatively low requirement for love. The safety and physiological needs are also relatively low. Consequently, the entrepreneur is "quickly" motivated by self-esteem since he has relatively few lower needs that must be satisfied, but his requirement for self-esteem is so great that*

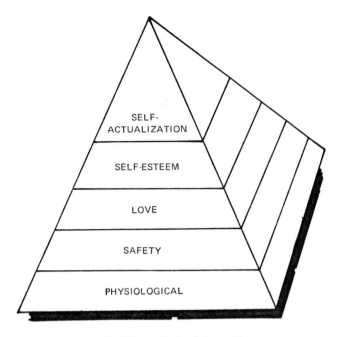

FIGURE 5. Maslow's Pyramid.

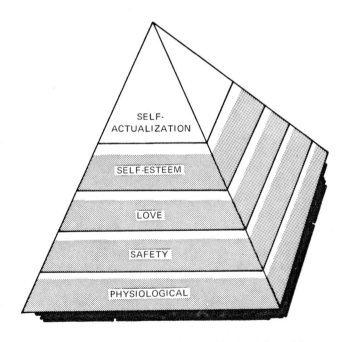

FIGURE 6. Theoretical Fulfillment of Maslow's Pyramid.

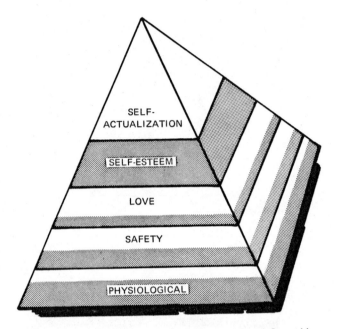

FIGURE 7. Entrepreneurial Fulfillment of Maslow's Pyramid.

it must be almost entirely satisfied before he can be motivated by self-actualization factors. The entrepreneur only perceives that his self-esteem has been satisfied when he has accomplished an extreme goal — his first million dollars, the $10,000,000 sales mark, or some other momentous event.

The first item on that list, "his first million dollars," is worth a few comments. The first-time entrepreneur *thinks* he is motivated by money; *he thinks* he wants a million dollars, but what happens when he achieves it — the exact same thing that happened to Andrew Carnegie. Carnegie often stated that as soon as he made a million dollars, he was going to quit. He made it at 30, then kept right on building. Entrepreneurs the first time around probably do not realize that their lives are fated to be one business start-up after another. *Building businesses, the achievement of creating an organization, is what makes the entrepreneur run. The money is just the way he proves to himself he is better than someone else. It is a way to keep score.*[6]

What happens then? When the entrepreneur has satisfied his self-esteem he is, according to Maslow, more likely to be motivated by self-actualization than by a lower need. This appears to be so. "There is the will. . . to succeed for the same, not of the fruits of success, but for success itself."[7] The man will continue to start up new ventures, new business, accept new challenges. Even though now independently wealthy, he still strives for self-actualization through new and exciting ventures. He may start to enjoy some of the finer things in life, indulge in some "self-improvement" sports (we shall discuss the competitive instinct in the entrepreneur in Chapter 5 and how that instinct is changed once self-esteem has been fulfilled), but the thrust of his momentum will be toward continuing his entrepreneurial endeavors.

In Maslow's model this behavior or these actions are quite understandable. For those individuals who have the need to conquer, who find great satisfaction in being successful entrepreneurs, once having achieved this state, it no longer serves as a motivator or satisfier. Satisfaction can only be achieved through renewed entrepreneurial activities.

For the man who has fulfilled his self-esteem needs, that is, once he has built a successful organization, building a business from scratch is a way of life. It's not only his occupation; it is also his vocation and his relaxation.

The classic example of the entrepreneurial breed probably is Sherman Fairchild. His father was a founder and the largest shareholder of International Business Machines. Obviously, every door at IBM was open to Sherman. He turned his back on the company. It was not that he scorned his father's money, but IBM was his father's baby, already grown to manhood. He wanted to build something he could proudly call his own. He founded Fairchild Camera & Instrument, then Fairchild Hiller Corporation, then Fairchild Recording Equipment. Money? What did he need money for, expecially after his father's death, when he became IBM's biggest stockholder? He had an urge to create, an urge that has grown stronger with the years.[8]

The Effective Entrepreneur, with minor exceptions, is focusing upon the first-time entrepreneur or the entrepreneur who has not yet fulfilled his self-esteem needs. He is not yet in the stage of "doing it for the sport of it." If we keep this brief discussion and the pyramid in Figure 7 in mind, it will help as we go over some of the other manifestations of entrepreneurial reality.

NOTES

[1] University of Toronto, School of Business, Tapes "Seminar on Venture Capital," Time, Inc., 1972

[2] Our thanks to Dr. Herbert Greenberg in his study of salesmen and managers. "The Right Man . . . The Right Job," Marketing Survey and Research Corporation, P.O. Box 2050, Research Park, Princeton, New Jersey, 08540. Dr. Greenberg developed the ego drive—empathy concept as it applies to sales and management personnel. Dr. Greenberg has developed a test that measures ego drive and empathy, that considers a great deal more "dynamics" than the oversimplified Swayne entrepreneur model, and rates an individual according to sales and management potential. The authors recommend the test (cost about $70) to potential entrepreneurs, as it will give insight into individual ego drive and empathy.

[3] "The Right Man," Marketing Survey and Research Corporation, New York, 1970, page 3.

[4] A. H. Maslow, *Motivation and Personality*, Harper & Row, 1954.

[5] Douglas McGregor, *The Human Side of Enterprise*, McGraw-Hill Book Co., Inc., 1960, pages 36–39.

[6] University of Toronto, School of Business, Tapes "Seminar on Venture Capital," Time, Inc., 1972.

[7] Peter Kilby, ed., *Entrepreneurship and Economic Development*, 1971, page 69.

[8] "The Incurables," *Forbes*, July 1, 1969, page 21.

4

THE ENTREPRENEUR'S MANAGEMENT PHILOSOPHY

In the introductory chapter, it was mentioned that one of the differentiating characteristics of entrepreneurs is their management philosophy and management methods. The purpose of this chapter is to examine these differences in detail.

As in the previous chapter, the authors are fortunate in being able to draw on a large reservoir of management literature and thought. The general approach taken has been to define briefly two major approaches to the study of the professional management process. These schools are the traditional or principles approach and the behaviorist approach. The entrepreneurial management process is then compared with these professional-management processes.

In this section several of these schools are described briefly and the successful entrepreneur is then compared to these schools or models. One of the major findings of the authors is that the entrepreneur manages differently than the professional manager. This is not to say that entrepreneurs are better or poorer managers; rather it is a reflection of a different environment in which entrepreneurs are found. As described previously, the professional manager is concerned primarily with maintenance of the present organization and gradual expansion of influence of his business. The entrepreneur on the other hand is concerned with creation, survival, and rapid initial growth. As a result, the style and techniques employed by the entrepreneur are different from those of the professional.

TRADITIONAL SCHOOL

The traditional school of management traces its origin to Fayol, a French manager of public utilities in the early 1900's. Most introductory courses in business management are still patterned after this approach.[1]

The primary thrust of this school is to break down the management process into five major functions. They are planning, organizing, staffing, directing, and controlling. Under each of these functions is found a list of activities that every professional manager must engage in to be successful. The particular business, its age, industrial environment, and a host of other factors determine how well it must perform these various activities in order to be successful. For example, General Motors devotes much time to and is very successful in forecasting future business trends, consumer tastes, coordinating employee effort, delegating authority, training new employees, developing performance standards and measuring results. While much effort is expended trying to motivate employees, G.M. has not been highly successful in this area, particularly with blue-collar employees. While success has not been achieved in this and other areas, overall success of G.M. is not dependent upon excellent motivation at the blue-collar level. The activities or capabilities critical to the success of G.M. lie in forecasting, coordinating, training, and implementation. What about entrepreneurs? What are their critical capabilities or activities? Are they the same as professional employees?

The following is a list of the five managerial functions and the various activities under each. This list was developed by R. Alec MacKenzie.[2] For each of the listed activities, there is an approximate evaluation of how well the entrepreneur performs them.

FUNCTION	ACTIVITY	DEFINITION	ENTREPRENEURIAL PERFORMANCE
			Poor Excellent
Planning	Forecast	Establish where present course will lead	
	Set Objectives	Determine desired end results	
	Develop Strategies	Decide how and when to achieve goals	
	Program	Establish priority sequence & timing of steps	
	Budget	Allocate resources	
	Set Procedures	Standardize methods	
	Develop Policies	Make standing decisions on important recurring matters	
Organizing	Establish Organization Structure	Draw up Organization Chart	
	Define Relationships	Define liaison lines to facilitate coordination	
	Create Position Descriptions	Define scope, relationships, responsibilities and authority	
	Establish Position Qualifications	Define qualifications for each person in each position	

FUNCTION	ACTIVITY	DEFINITION	ENTREPRENEURIAL PERFORMANCE (Poor → Excellent)
Staffing	Select	Recruit qualified people for each position	(bar ~90% filled)
	Orient	Familiarize new people with the situation	(bar ~10% filled)
	Train	Make proficient by instruction and practice	(bar ~30% filled)
	Develop	Help improve knowledge, attitudes, and skills	(bar ~75% filled)
Directing	Delegate	Assign responsibility and exact accountability for results	(bar ~40% filled)
	Motivate	Persuade and inspire people to take desired action	(bar 100% filled)
	Coordinate	Relate efforts in most effective coordination	(bar ~35% filled)
	Manage Differences	Encourage independent thought and resolve conflicts	(bar ~40% filled)
	Manage Change	Stimulate creativity and innovations in achieving goals	(bar 100% filled)
Controlling	Establish Reporting System	Determine what critical data are needed, how and when	(bar ~60% filled)
	Develop Performance Standards	Set conditions that will exist when key duties are well done	(bar ~20% filled)
	Measure Results	Ascertain extent of deviation from goals and standards	(bar ~55% filled)
	Take Corrective Action	Adjust plans, counsel to attain standards, replan	(bar ~70% filled)
	Reward	Praise, remunerate and discipline	(bar 100% filled)

In summary, we find the entrepreneur to be a fair to good planner. *He will devote little time to organizing and staffing except in selecting good personnel. The entrepreneur knows how to motivate his people and remains highly flexible.* He is also effective in the control function particularly with respect to people.

As for overall evaluation of the entrepreneur, one of his critical capabilities is employee leadership.

BEHAVIORIST SCHOOL

Since the initial motivational studies at Western Electric in the 1930's, behavioral scientists have played an increasing role in management theory. Large corporations frequently employ industrial psychologists on their staff to assist in determining management personnel policy.

Two common definitions of management point out the difference between the traditional and behaviorists schools. The traditional-school definition of management is "the economic allocation of resources, i.e., land, labor, and capital." The behaviorist definition is "achieving results through people."

The behaviorists, as implied by the definition, are mainly concerned with the behavior of individuals within an organization. They are concerned with the behavior of both employer and employee that results in high productivity. Several distinguished authors have developed models to help explain or categorize management styles and management philosophies. On the following pages the reader will find how the entrepreneur fits some of the more well-known models.

McGREGOR — THEORY X — THEORY Y

Professor Douglas McGregor developed his theory by describing two extreme management styles, X and Y.[3] The theory X style makes the following assumptions about employee behavior:

> 1. The average human being has an inherent dislike of work and will avoid it if he can.
>
> 2. Therefore, most people must be coerced, controlled, di-

rected, and threatened with punishment if management is to get them to put forth adequate effort toward the achievement of organizational objectives.

3. The average human prefers to be directed, wishes to avoid responsibility, has relatively little ambition, and wants security above all.

These assumptions converted into management behavior are found to some extent on the contemporary American business scene. Ed Reddig of White Consolidated Industries, however, closely approaches this philosophy in dealing with newly acquired companies. His classical action is to extinguish his cigarettes in subordinates' full cups of coffee.

Theory Y management philosophies are as follows:

1. The expenditure of physical and mental effort in work is as natural as play or rest.

2. External control and the threat of punishment are not the only means of bringing about effect toward organizational objectives. Man will exercise self-direction and self-control in the service of objectives to which he is committed.

3. Commitment to objectives is a function of rewards associated with their achievement.

4. The average human being learns, under proper conditions, not only to accept but to seek responsibility.

5. The capacity to exercise a relatively high degree of imagination, ingenuity, and creativity in the solution of organizational problems is widely, not narrowly, distributed in the population.

6. Under the conditions of modern industrial life, the intellectual potentialities of the average human being are only partially utilized.

The reader can easily discern that the theory Y philosophy is oriented more toward encouraging employee participation in the management process. Theory Y, however, should not be interpreted

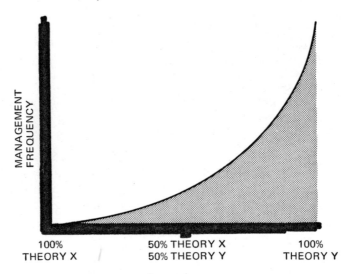

FIGURE 8. McGregor — Professional Management.

to mean that the boss is only a nice guy. Rather, a theory Y manager can carry a hatchet as well as a magic wand. The use of terms such as participative management, management by objectives, and job enrichment all represent management's increasing acceptance of theory Y and the behaviorist school of management.

If we imagine the theory X — theory Y attitude toward people as a spectrum ranging from 100% acceptance and implementation of theory X, to some midpoint where a manager believes and acts according to a little of both attitudes, all the way to 100% acceptance and implementation of theory Y, we may then examine how managers fit McGregor's profile. Figure 8 illustrates how many behavioral theorists believe management should act.

Actually, most professional managers lie somewhere between the two extremes. In recent years, the trend has been to move in the Y direction.

Entrepreneurs, on the other hand, tend not to lie at an intermediate place on the scale. Rather, *most entrepreneurs are found at or near one of the extremes. They are either theory X or theory Y managers and not in between.* Figure 9 shows this relationship. Neither theory X nor theory Y seems to be a better entrepreneurial style.

With the increasing education of youthful entrepreneurs to the fact that there is such a thing as theory Y, we should expect that future entrepreneurs will be either theory X or theory Y, but there will be a greater propensity toward theory Y.

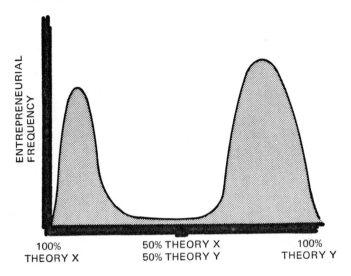

FIGURE 9. McGregor — Entrepreneurial Management.

BLAKE — MANAGERIAL GRID

The Managerial Grid as developed by Blake, et al.,[4] describes managerial behavior based upon two variables. One reflects concern for production or output; the other variable, concern for people. In this instance, their term "concern for" refers to the degree of concern, not the actual results. That is, it does not represent real production or the extent to which human-relationship needs are actually met. It does indicate managerial concern for production and/or people and how these influence each other.

These two variables and some of their possible combinations are shown in Figure 10. The horizontal axis indicates concern for production, and the vertical axis indicates concern for people. Each is expressed on a scale ranging from 1, which represents minimal concern, to 9, which represents maximal concern.

Briefly, the lower left corner of the grid diagram in Figure 10 shows a 1, 1 style. This represents minimal concern for production and minimal concern for people. The 1, 9 style in the upper left corner depicts maximal concern for people but minimal concern for production. The 9, 1 style in the lower right corner portrays maximal concern for production and minimal concern for human relationships. The 9, 9 style in the upper righthand corner represents maximum concern for both human relationships and production. The 5, 5 style in the center of the diagram is "middle of the road" in both areas of concern.

1,1 MANAGEMENT

EXERTION OF MINIMUM EFFORT TO GET REQUIRED WORK DONE IS APPROPRIATE TO SUSTAIN ORGANIZATION MEMBERSHIP

1,9 MANAGEMENT

THOUGHTFUL ATTENTION TO NEEDS OF PEOPLE FOR SATISFYING RELATIONSHIPS LEADS TO A COMFORTABLE FRIENDLY ORGANIZATION ATMOSPHERE AND WORK TEMPO

9,9 MANAGEMENT

WORK ACCOMPLISHMENT IS FROM COMMITTED PEOPLE INTER-DEPENDENCE THROUGH A "COMMON STAKE" IN ORGANIZATION PURPOSE LEADS TO RELATIONSHIPS OF TRUST AND RESPECT

9,1 MANAGEMENT

EFFICIENCY IN OPERATIONS RESULTS FROM ARRANGING CONDITIONS OF WORK IN SUCH A WAY THAT HUMAN ELEMENTS INTERFERE TO A MINIMUM DEGREE

5,5 MANAGEMENT

ADEQUATE ORGANIZATION PERFORMANCE IS POSSIBLE THROUGH BALANCING THE NECESSITY TO GET OUT WORK WHILE MAINTAINING MORALE OF PEOPLE AT A SATISFACTORY LEVEL

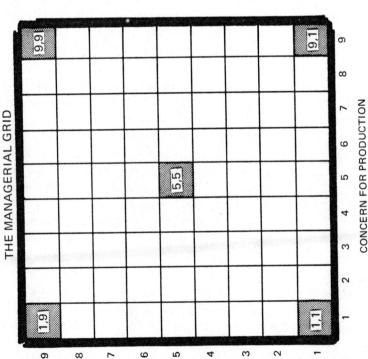

THE MANAGERIAL GRID

CONCERN FOR PEOPLE

CONCERN FOR PRODUCTION

FIGURE 10. Managerial Grid.

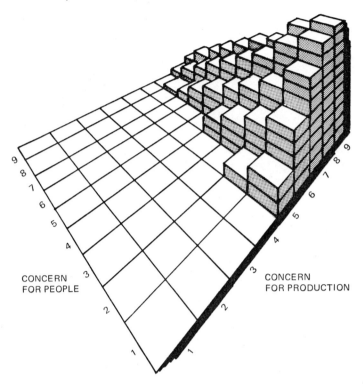

FIGURE 11. Entrepreneurial Distribution on Managerial Grid.

The behavioral theorists say that once managers have been able to place themselves on the managerial grid, they may then make a conscientious effort to work toward the 9, 9 organizational climate. In other words, the behavioral theorists believe all good managers will fall in the 9, 9 square and that anything less is inappropriate for all concerned. This may be true for mature organizations using professional management techniques, but it is not so for the entrepreneur. The entrepreneur, we must remember, is fighting for survival. He must be more concerned with production than with people; if he is not, he will more than likely end up as a bankrupt entrepreneur. The authors do not mean that it is not right, proper, and moral for a manager to be highly concerned with his people, but successful entrepreneurs, both by necessity and by basic personality, must make decisions clearly in favor of production over people. If they did not do so, the organization would not grow into the mature organization that is needed to support the proper concern for its people.

Figure 11 illustrates the distribution of 100 entrepreneurs on the Managerial Grid. Concern for people to some degree is profitable and

SATISFIERS
(MOTIVATORS)

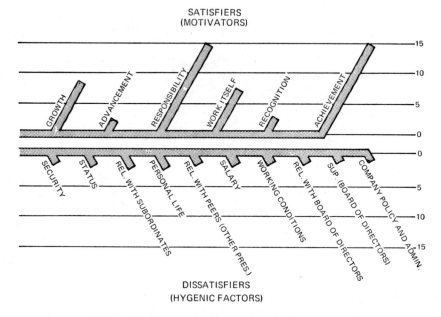

DISSATISFIERS
(HYGENIC FACTORS)

FIGURE 12. Herzberg's Model — How the Entrepreneur Fits.

certainly in certain entrepreneurial adventures absolutely essential, but in the majority of cases, *the concern for production is overwhelming.*

HERZBERG

Professor Frederick Herzberg, distinguished professor of management at the University of Utah, has done an extensive analysis of those factors that motivate employees.[5] From his research he has found that the degree of job satisfaction is a function of two sets of factors. They are "motivators" and "dissatisfiers."

Motivators, for the most part, are the factors of achievement, recognition, responsibility, growth, advancement, and other matters associated with the self-actualization of the individual on the job. Job satisfaction and high production were associated with motivators, while disappointments and ineffectiveness were usually associated with dissatisfiers.

Dissatisfiers are made up, essentially, of such matters as pay, supplemental benefits, company policy and administration, behavior of supervision, working conditions, and several other factors somewhat peripheral to the task. Though traditionally perceived by management as motivators of people, these factors were found to be more potent as dissatisfiers. High motivation does not result from their improvement, but dissatisfaction does result from their deterioration. Negative motivators can be dissatisfiers too, but not so frequently as the factors just given. For example, while achievement is a motivator, failure to achieve can, of course, be a dissatisfier.

Figure 12 presents a theoretical distribution of motivators and dissatisfiers for entrepreneurs. Note the relative importance of achievement and responsibility. Non-entrepreneur corporate presidents differ from entrepreneurs in the relative importance of these two factors; for the non-entrepreneur corporation president, achievement plays a less important role in their psychological make-up. For entrepreneurs, *achievement or ego-drive is an all-consuming motivator*. The relative importance of most of the other satisfiers is a function of the man's ego drive/empathy balance and intensity.

Entrepreneurs, like most corporate officials, are little affected by the common dissatisfier such as salary. Motivators, particularly achievement and responsibility, far outweigh such dissatisfaction. By asking various groups of employees to describe those things that give them satisfaction and dissatisfaction, it has been possible to discover and determine the relative importance of many common satisfiers and dissatisfiers. It has been found that different groups, e.g. presidents, engineers, and clerks are motivated by or dissatisfied by these items in varying degrees. For example, Figure 13 shows a distribution of the importance of these factors for an average group of factory employees such as mechanics. The important point to remember is that unless the dissatisfiers, such as company policy and supervision, are not reasonably fulfilled, the satisfiers cannot be effectively used as motivators.

What motivates an entrepreneur? Is it money? Status? Recognition? Or does he climb the mountain just because it is there? Observations indicate that he is motivated not by money, safety, or love. His motivator is his unique ego drive, balanced with empathy or ability to read others. Maslow would define his motivation as ego and self-fulfillment. Herzberg would define it as achievement, responsibility, and growth. Of course, the yardstick for measurement is money; that, however, is not the major motivator!

Of almost equal significance is how the entrepreneur views his employees, relative to the Herzberg model. This view does not distinquish between those satisfiers and dissatisfiers of Herzberg. Instead,

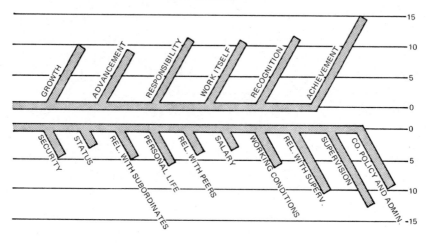

SATISFIERS
(MOTIVATORS)

DISSATISFIERS
(HYGENIC FACTORS)

FIGURE 13. Herzberg's Model — How Many Workers Fit.

*he tends to view all as a motivator, to some degree or another, with
salary being in the entrepreneur's opinion, the greatest motivator.*
Figure 14 illustrates how the entrepreneur believes his employees
are motivated.

At this point, the reader should be impressed with the major
focus of the cited authors. The main point is that entrepreneurs
are motivated by an inner need to achieve — a self-esteem need.
Money, financial security, and public recognition are but a few motivations commonly mentioned. It is the author's contention that these
are only outward manifestations of the man's basic needs — self-
esteem and achievement.

STOGDILL

For entrepreneurs, the achievement motive is very closely related to
a strong desire for freedom of action or lack of restricting forces.
This motivating force of freedom is frequently cited by entrepreneurs under dissatisfaction when working in large businesses. This dissatisfaction frequently manifests itself in low productivity. For the
potential entrepreneur, the best way to raise his productivity is to

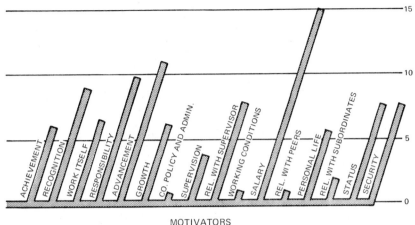

MOTIVATORS

FIGURE 14. Herzberg's Model — How the Entrepreneur
Views His Employees.

start his own business where the restricting forces will be reduced.
They will never be eliminated because the government, society,
creditors, customers, and equity interests always restrict his freedom
of action to some degree.

The relationship between freedom of action and productivity
has been studied extensively by psychologists and sociologists.[6]
They have found that a level of freedom exists for each job and
individual where productivity is greatest. For example, productivity
is greatest for certain production-line jobs where freedom is least
and for research scientists where freedom is greatest. Figure 15
represents the relationship between productivity and freedom for
an intermediate type position, such as secretaries or clerks.

In contrast, research scientists, with very high achievement
motives and a strong desire for personal responsibility of their
actions demand an environment where freedom of action is at a
maximum.

The freedom–productivity curve for the group is represented in
Figure 16. In this respect, entrepreneurs are very much like scientists, doctors, and university professors.

SUMMARY

In summary, we find that the primary motivating force associated
with entrepreneurial activity is defined in various ways. It has been

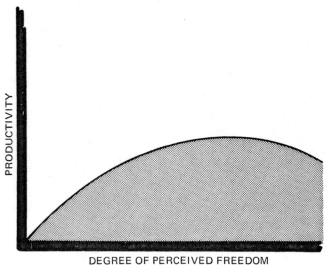

FIGURE 15. Stogdill's Theory.

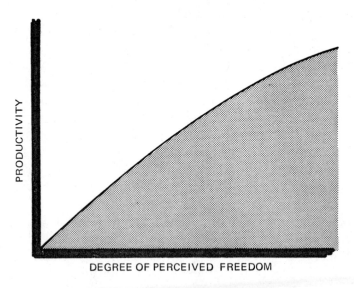

FIGURE 16. Stogdill's Theory — How the Entrepreneur Fits.

called ego drive, need to achieve, and self-esteem need. These definitions all revolve around the central theme of an inner desire to accomplish a difficult task well. Entrepreneurs are motivated by an
intense desire in this direction.

It is interesting to note that many feel that the major motivation is money. We have found, however, that money is merely a measure of accomplishment, not the primary motivator. Common definitions of this motivating force include the desire to do a good job and the search for community recognition.

The authors contend that the uncertain nature of a new business and the entrepreneur's continual fight for survival result in management philosophies that differ from professional managers. When compared with the more traditional schools of management, we find the entrepreneur to be:

1. A fair to good planner

2. A poor organizer

3. Good at selecting subordinates

4. Good at motivating his subordinates

5. Very effective in the control function

When compared with the behaviorists school of management, we find the entrepreneur to be a man of extremes. On the McGregor X–Y scale, he tends to be either X or Y and not at an intermediate position. On Blake's management grid, he tends to have a high concern for production with varying concern for people. He tends to place great emphasis on salary as a motivator for his subordinates and will also use the job as a motivator.

In the next chapter, entrepreneurs are characterized in another critical aspect. The major concern will be the identification of the set of behavioral patterns that characterize entrepreneurs.

NOTES

[1] See Koontz & O'Donnell, *Principles of Management.*

[2] Alec R. MacKenzie, "The Management Process in 3-D", Harvard Business Review, (November-December 1969) p. 80.

[3] Excerpts from Douglas McGregor, *The Human Side of Entreprise,* McGraw Hill Book Co., Inc., 1960.

[4] "Breakthrough in Organization Development" *Harvard Business Review*, Nov–Dec. 1964.

[5] Frederick Herzberg, "One More Time: How do you Motivate Employees?" How Successful Executives Handle People, *Harvard Business Review,* 1970, pages 82–91.

[6] Ralph M. Stogdill, *Individual Behavior and Group Achievement,* Oxford University Press, Inc., 1969, Chapter 5.

5

ENTREPRENEURIAL CHARACTERISTICS

PERSONALITY

In an attempt to predict who will be successful managers and sales-men, psychologists have tried for a number of years to uncover unique personality characteristics. Attempts have been made to correlate success with such characteristics as aggressiveness, clever-ness, honesty, or analytical ability.

Reference to the Boy Scout Oath will provide a long list of characteristics from which to choose. Others have tried personal characteristics such as height, weight, age, baldness, and others.

Nearly all such attempts have proved fruitless. The difficulties in defining and measuring such characteristics as honesty are insur-mountable.

In addition, there is apparently little or no correlation between many of these characteristics and success.

One of the most rigorous attempts to develop a usable guideline for predicting success has been accomplished by Dr. D. W. Merrill.[1] Most of his research has been with salesmen and he has achieved a fair degree of predictive power.

Merrill's technique has been to measure social style by two per-sonality characteristics, assertiveness and objectivity. Assertiveness is defined as the degree of effort an individual makes to influence the thinking and actions of others.

A scale containing adjectives ranging from aggressive and bold to reserved and quiet represents this characteristic. A high rating on this scale suggests that the person being described is seen as pushy and over-eager to influence others. A very low rating on this scale suggests that the person being described is seen as quiet and unas-suming in his relationships with others.

The following scale shows the difference between high or low assertiveness.

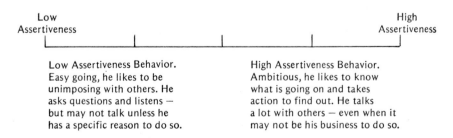

The second characteristic of social style, objectivity, is defined as the degree of effort an individual makes to be unemotional and self-controlled in his relationship with others.

A scale containing 80 adjectives ranging from cold and tough to personable and emotional represents this characteristic. A high rating on this scale suggests that the person being described is seen as objective and harsh in his relationships. A very low rating on this scale suggests that he is seen as soft-hearted and sensitive in his relationships.

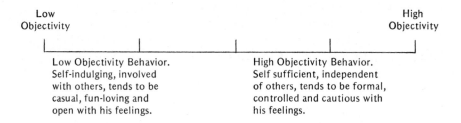

Low
Objectivity

High
Objectivity

Low Objectivity Behavior.
Self-indulging, involved
with others, tends to be
casual, fun-loving and
open with his feelings.

High Objectivity Behavior.
Self sufficient, independent
of others, tends to be formal,
controlled and cautious with
his feelings.

The two measures of social style are superimposed one on the other to define four different styles as shown in the Figure 17.

Beginning in the upper right quadrant and moving clockwise, the four styles can be described as follows:[2]

> 1. The driving style — This is the TELL/CONTROL INDI-
> VIDUAL. He is highly assertive and highly objective. He
> makes an effort to tell people with his assertiveness and to
> control himself with his objectivity. He is task oriented — a
> "head" type guy. His style is called DRIVING. He is the
> control specialist because he combines personal power and
> emotional control in his relationships.
>
> 2. The expressive style — This is the TELL/EMOTE INDI-
> VIDUAL. He is highly assertive, too, but is lower in objec-
> tivity. Like the driving style, he makes an effort to tell
> people with his assertiveness, but places more importance
> on the relationships than on the tasks. Rather than trying to
> control his emotional expressiveness, he is more impulsive.
> He is a "gut" type guy, more intuitive than the driving. His
> style is called EXPRESSIVE. He is a social specialist because
> he combines personal power with emotional expression in
> his relationships.
>
> 3. The amiable style — This is the ASK/EMOTE individual.
> He is low in assertiveness and low in objectivity. Like the
> expressive type, he softens his style with a more personal,

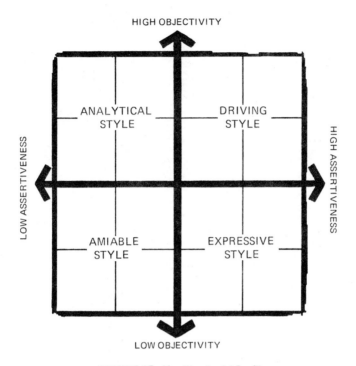

FIGURE 17. Merrill — Social Profile.

feeling approach. He is a non-aggressive "gut" type guy. He possesses the AMIABLE style. He is the supportive specialist because he combines personal reserve with emotional expression in his relationships.

4. The analytical style — This is the ASK/CONTROL individual. He is low in assertiveness but high in objectivity. He is as objective and task oriented as the driving type, but like the amiable, he softens his style with low assertiveness. Rather than being directive, he is more asking of others. He is a "head" type guy who is more asking of others. He is a "head" type guy who is more reserved with people. His style is called ANALYTICAL. He is the technical specialist because he combines personal reserve with emotional control in his relationships.

Dr. Merrill's results indicate that successful salesmen fall, with the exception of end points, with about equal distribution all over the graph. Few successful salesmen are extremely one way or the other.

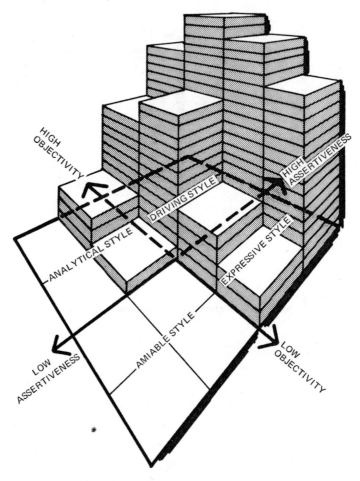

FIGURE 18. Merrill — How the Entrepreneur Fits.

In summary, Dr. Merrill states:

> "There is no such thing as a good or bad social style when it comes to getting along with others satisfactorily. It is more a matter of how you use your style to help others discover their needs that determines whether or not you'll succeed in building a productive relationship with another person."

This seems to indicate that almost anyone can be a good salesman if he learns how to effectively use his own style.

How about entrepreneurs? Can the same be said? That is, can anyone be an effective entrepreneur if he learns to use his own style effectively?

Or, do entrepreneurs have unique personality characteristics?

Experience indicates that there is a definite relationship between social style and entrepreneurial success. A plot of the distribution of 100 entrepreneurs is presented in Figure 18.

Personality characteristics associated with high assertiveness are obviously necessary. With respect to objectivity, no definite relationship is apparent except possibly a tendency toward a middle position.

In summary, what kind of a picture have we drawn of an entrepreneur? He is a strong manager who takes very active participation in his business. He is good at planning, selecting his employees, and motivating them. His management style is either highly autocratic or highly participative with the major concern for production. A unique characteristic is to combine his motivation ability with concern for production. In his dealings with others, he is very assertive. This is the picture of the entrepreneur we have painted. Let us now discuss some specific characteristics.*

INTELLIGENCE

A man must be intelligent to be an effective entrepreneur. This is a quality all entrepreneurs possess. Entrepreneurial effectiveness increases in proportion to intelligence. Logically enough, there is a range of diminishing returns, beyond which the ability to get the job done is reduced. Figure 19 illustrates this relationship.

It is interesting to note that Ned Heiser, president of the Heiser Corporation, an $80 million venture capital corporation, states that most effective entrepreneurs "have a very high IQ, and they are doers." Mr. Heiser charts potential entrepreneurs on a two-axis scale. On one axis, a man's intelligence is plotted, and on the other, the degree of work the man is doing is plotted. What Mr. Heiser is obviously looking for is an intelligent doer, but he states very clearly a warning to all venture capitalists: "The guy we really have to watch out for is a 'dumb doer'."[3]

POSITIVE ATTITUDE — SELF-CONFIDENCE

"I am going to be the president," not "I would like to be the president."

*Some of these characteristics have been identified by the J. W. Newman Corporation in their pamphlet, "What's The Difference?", 1970, the J. W. Newman Corporation, 4311 Wilshire Blvd., Los Angeles, California 90005.

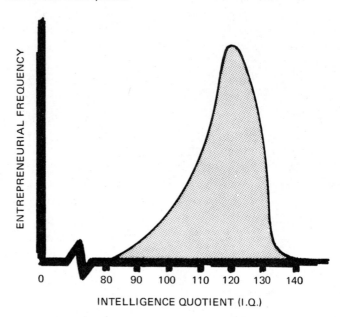

FIGURE 19. Entrepreneurial Intelligence Distribution.

The importance of a positive attitude and self-confidence has long been recognized as one of the keys to success. Following are a few quotes that emphasize this point.

> "*If you persuade yourself that you can do a certain thing, provided this thing be possible, you will do it, however difficult it may be.* If on the contrary, you imagine that you cannot do the simplest thing in the world, it is impossible for you to do it, and molehills become for you unscalable mountains." — *Emile Coue*

> "The high expectations of superior entrepreneurs are based primarily on what they think about themselves — about their own ability to select, train, and motivate their subordinates. What an entrepreneur thinks about himself [sic] subtly influences what he believes about his subordinates, what he expects of them, and how he treats them. If he has the confidence in his ability to develop and stimulate them to high levels of performance, he will expect much of them and will treat them with confidence so that his expectations will be met . . . Stated in another [way], *the entrepreneur's expectations create credibility.* As a consequence, his subordinates accept his expectations as realistic and try hard to achieve them."

The man never feels that he has the inability to do anything. Once he establishes a goal, he is *not concerned with whether the goal will be reached but rather only how to reach it.* His vocabulary does not have words such as "should" or "try" but rather "will."

He has abiding faith that guides his own destiny. Accordingly, there is every reason for him to believe that today and tomorrow will be bright, productive, and profitable. With this extreme confidence, he naturally exudes extreme enthusiasm about where he and his company are going.

An incurable optimist, he has a tendency to avoid anything that brings him sadness. Bad news stops with him and good news is spread. Even when times are tough, the man will play the success role although his business is not going as well as his action plan called for.

A man who has this type of optimism, determination, and confidence, whether he is an entrepreneur or not, is the man that can be picked out easily in a crowd or meeting. To those who do not share this sparkle, he will excite in them a combination of envy, respect, and admiration.

The reader may expect that due to their very positive, confident outlook, entrepreneurs are extroverts. In general, this is true. Figure 20 shows the relationship of behavior to entrepreneurship. The curve is skewed in favor of extroverts, as one might expect.

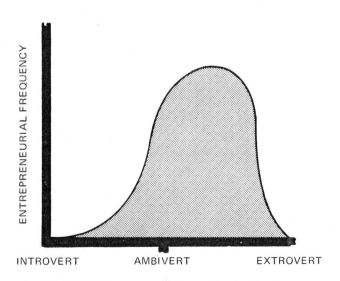

FIGURE 20. Entrepreneurial Personality Distribution.

Is this a learned trait or is it inherited? Dale Carnegie has shown that it can be learned. He found that the key to learning self-confidence was the desire and the ability to communicate with others.

Thousands can attribute this success to various public-speaking courses or to mutual self-help organizations such as Toastmasters. Many coprorations now provide educational opportunities in this area for their employees. This, of course, leads us to the conclusion that most successful entrepreneurs are effective public speakers. One of the commonly cited reasons for failure, be it social, individual, business or government is the inability of people to communicate. Thus we see that *the entrepreneur with his strong empathy level is usually a good communicator.*

An extrovert and an incurable optimist, the man exudes his confidence and the feeling that "we're going to make it really big." His positive attitude is quickly passed on to those around him. This positive communicativeness is one of the major reasons he can move others into action. *As Henry Ford stated, "Whether you think you can or you think you can't, you're right."*

GOAL ORIENTATION

Three bricklayers were once asked "What are you doing?" The first replied, "I trowel mortar on bricks and put them in place," the second replied, "I am building a wall," and the third, "I am helping to build a church where people can worship the Lord." Only the third bricklayer was goal oriented. His labors were guided by a place of worship while the other two could not see beyond the activities of placing bricks and building walls.

To paraphrase Dr. George S. Ordione, a leading proponent of the "Management by Objectives" school, one of the most critical problems facing industry today is that policies, procedures, and rules have oriented employees to think only in terms of their daily activities. The goals for which these activities were established have been lost.

The reader will recall that in the first part of Chapter 4, entrepreneurs were defined as fair to good planners. They are particularly good business and personal goal setters! These goals in turn are related to their underlying motivational makeup as discussed in Chapter 3.

The goals of the entrepreneur usually have some definite characteristics. They are quantifiable or measurable so that he knows how close he is coming to achieving them. The goals are also realistic in that they are possible, although not easy, to achieve.

For ease in understanding this concept, the reader should visualize a ship at sea headed for a foreign port. The captain would change the position of the rudder to achieve his goal, i.e., port. An activity-centered captain would be more interested in the appearance of the ship and following standard operating procedures than in directing.

The practical result of this goal orientation is that the entrepreneur is *not so much interested as to why a mistake was made, but what can be done to correct the mistake and get back on the track.* While constantly sensing success, he makes every present moment count in some way toward his goal. This future orientation produces very little talk about things and accomplishments of the past, but rather a preoccupation of what has to be done today to achieve his future goals.

A spin-off of both forms of the entrepreneur's goals is that he intuitively finds himself putting into practice one of Drucker's finest principles: "Maximization of opportunities is a meaningful, indeed a precise, definition of the entrepreneurial job. It implies that *effectiveness rather than efficiency is essential in business. The pertinent question is not how to do things right, but how to find the right things to do,* and to concentrate resources and efforts on them." The entrepreneur, then, by the very nature of having precise, quantified, visual goals naturally concentrates on things that are important and puts his talents and the talents of his organization to work on them. He is not concerned with doing everything 100% correctly.

ACTION ORIENTATION

"There are three kinds of people — those who make things happen, those who stand by and watch, and those who don't know."

Entrepreneurs are people who make things happen!

Goal orientation and action orientation are very closely related concepts. Both are necessary for success. While goal orientation refers to the establishment of goals and the ability to keep all activities consistent with these goals, action orientation refers to the type and time frame of the decisions made to achieve goals. At one extreme is Mr. Milktoast, who, when a problem develops or when a deviation is detected from the planned course, rationalizes his way out of the problem, takes no corrective action, and continues with his normal activities. At the other extreme is Mr. Fly-Off-The-Handle, who, when a problem develops, immediately sees it as critical and immediately takes drastic action to correct it even though it may not be warranted.

Most decisions in the business world are not made at either of these two extremes. Most large and established organizations have staffs to detect these problems before they become critical. Resources are also available to permit a solution to be agreed upon and implemented with relative ease. Only rarely is drastic action required such as that taken by Townsend at Chrysler when he laid off 30 percent of the staff in one month.

Entrepreneurs, however, face an entirely different environment. The major difference is that they usually have limited resources at their disposal. For example, they usually do not have the cash resources to withstand a sustained deviation from plan. Similarly, they do not have a trained planning staff available to detect problems or to evaluate alternative solutions. The truly exceptional entrepreneur is a man who can evaluate the effect of deviations and determine the appropriate action in a short period of time with limited information.

In the real world, we do not see this idealized man very often. Rather, most successful entrepreneurs are more action oriented.

He must not only do the job and do the job right, but he must do the job right now. He has developed the habit of responding to the present moment. The entrepreneur does not react quickly just because it is a matter of true life or death for his company, but rather because he wants to react. He gets a feeling of excitement, intensity, and urgency. It gives him a sense of power, motion, and accomplishment. This action, this motion creates the same type of envy and respect as the positive attitude we previously discussed, especially among those whose position in life allows for a more cautious approach to accomplishing objectives.

For those not accustomed to being or working in an action environment, they may mistake the "Nowness" of an entrepreneur for impulsiveness. *Entrepreneurs do tend to make management decisions too quickly from an omniscient point of view, but more important, rapid decision making and implementation is essential to any new organization, else the company dies of procrastination.*

To illustrate how the reaction of entrepreneurs differs from that of executives of large mature organizations, suppose that an entrepreneur and a professional executive are faced with the same problem.

The professional executive learns that gross margins are far below those programmed and that further examination shows direct labor to be the cost category that is causing the loss. In other words, the production people are not completing the jobs in the time budgeted. The professional president would probably assign someone (or a task force) to study the cause for the discrepancy. The study would probably include a review of time standards, working conditions, labor relations, employee morale, and other pertinent (and sometimes not so pertinent) areas of concern. Once the study were complete, a course of action would be implemented that would have a high probability of success. Figure 21 below illustrates the professional solution to the problem. The desired solution is fairly well defined; it takes a relatively long period of time to accomplish; it is accomplished within fairly narrow guidelines; and the actual course of action is well controlled and has few setbacks.

Entrepreneurial management calls for a different response. The entrepreneur may immediately fire some people or perhaps immediately increase prices. In any event, his response to the problem will be immediate, most often intuitive, and may not have an extremely high probability of success. Figure 22 illustrates an example of entrepreneurial management's solution to a problem. Note the immediate response, the wide guidelines (which may even be exceeded), the relatively wide area of an acceptable solution (relative to Figure 21), and the erratic course of action.

An important point must be emphasized at this juncture. That is, both the professional president and the entrepreneurial president are doing what is proper for their organization. The professional president must make many trade-offs regarding his company's long-term future and must, by necessity, be cautious about finding and implementing solutions. The entrepreneur, on the other hand, has developed a short-run consciousness while being unconsciously oriented toward the long-term future of his organization. He is more concerned with survival, not five years from now, but next week. He must react and act quickly to keep his firm alive. As one might expect, *the professional president would not last long in an entrepreneurial envi-*

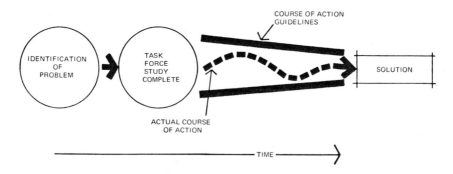

FIGURE 21. Solution to Problem — Professional Management.

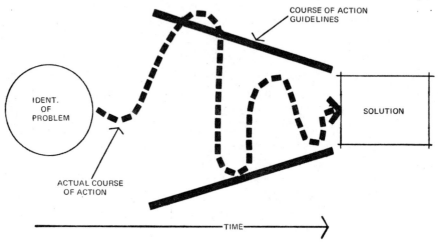

FIGURE 22. Solution to Problem — Entrepreneurial
Management.

*ronment and, likewise, the entrepreneurial president would cause
havoc in a large, mature organization.*

RISK-TAKING ATTITUDE

"It is never safe to look into the future with eyes of fear."

Development of a theory of decision making has been one of the
preoccupations of business schools in recent years. One aspect of the
research has been the determination of an individual's attitude toward
risk and how this attitude affects his decision making.

It is generally conceded that Las Vegas gamblers are risk seekers.
That is, while the expected return from gambling is negative, they
seek to gamble for the large potential gain. Most people, including
business executives, on the other hand, are generally agreed to be
risk-neutral to risk-adverse. That is, they would only accept a gamble
in which the expected return was neutral. The reader is cautioned to
recognize the limits of such a model as this. It has been found, for
example, that an individual's attitude changes as the potential gain
and loss vary with respect to his wealth.

Many would argue that entrepreneurs are risk seekers. They
would point to the large number of failures as opposed to the few
numbers of outstanding successes to support their point, vis-à-vis —
Walt Disney. He went bankrupt three times before "making it."

One can more easily argue however, that entrepreneurs are not risk seekers. Rather *they are risk-neutral to risk-adverse.* Successful entrepreneurs have the ability to evaluate their own abilities and to read the environment, the people involved, the market and evaluate accurately the risks involved. *They only undertake those businesses that offer them a positive expected return.* This is not to say that a high degree of risk does not exist. In some cases the entrepreneur will take a high risk if the potential return is high enough. In almost all cases he can evaluate the risks and decrease them to manageable proportions.

At this juncture, the effect of business schools and consulting firms should be mentioned. Various sophisticated analytical tools have been developed that allow the entrepreneur and business firms in general to effectively evaluate the degree of risk involved in a project. Some of the more important tools include statistical analysis, market research techniques, simulation, operations research, and decision theory. Large business firms employ entire staff departments to evaluate new ventures on a continuing basis. One of the reasons for the rise in franchising has been the ability of the franchisors to concentrate on the risks associated with their product or service. This knowledge is then passed on to the franchisee to help him skirt many of the potential pitfalls.

Before leaving the subject of risk, it should be pointed out that research done by John W. Atkinson of the University of Michigan indicates that the entrepreneurs can use the high-risk environment as a motivator. He found that the degree of motivation of workers is related to the probability of success of the venture. If the probability of success is viewed to be around .50, workers have the strongest motivation. As the probability of success increases or decreases from this point, motivation declines.[4] Figure 23 portrays this idea graphically.

THICK SKINNED

"I don't get ulcers; I give them."

An absolute requirement of every entrepreneur, and perhaps of every successful president, is that the man have a psychologically thick epidermis strong enough to protect him against ego threats. By his position in the marketplace, the entrepreneur is constantly subjected to emotional tension from customers, board of directors, employees,

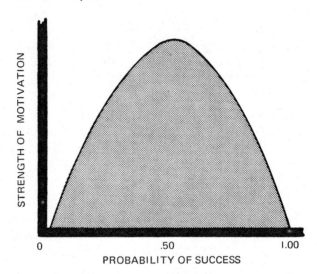

FIGURE 23. Atkinson — Risk and Motivation.

competitors, on-lookers, well-wishers, those who are envious, and to the constant fact that the actual performance seldom goes as planned. For those not cut out to be entrepreneurs, the constant emotional assaults quickly penetrate the emotional skin and prove devastating to the ego, producing permanent scars to the personality.

In large organizations, the president may often turn to those around him, both internal and external to his company, who are on the same intellectual plane he is. This outlet, this emotional hand-holding, is seldom a privilege available to entrepreneurs. Any president's job is lonely, but the entrepreneur's is more so. It is not enough to say that *he must be able to stand up under the pressure and loneliness of the position, but that he must thrive on it.* He must actually enjoy it. When deadlines close in, when a decision affecting the entire future of the organization is needed, when every conceivable pressure grows more severe, the entrepreneur must actually function more efficiently, more smoothly. *He is conditioned to become more excited under pressure.*

Many appear to be immersed in work. They work fast. Many are early risers, late workers, or both. The man is completely willing to make any sacrifices necessary to make the business go. Along with this high degree of business energy, the entrepreneur, by necessity, is probably in good physical shape. With the physical stamina, he lives up to "When the going gets tough, the tough get going." Many have one gear — fastest. In addition to his immersion in work, there

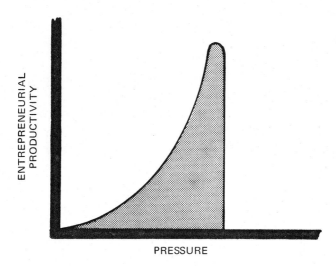

FIGURE 24. Entrepreneurial Productivity and Pressure.

is a natural nonvaluing of leisure. In other words, *work and fun are synonymous.*

As the pressure increases, so does his output. Figure 24 illustrates the relationship of the entrepreneurial productivity to pressure (both external and internal). One conclusion of the graph is clear. There is a breaking point. The external pressures are seldom enough to push the man to the breaking point, but when combined with his own internal self-generated pressure, the entrepreneur tends to push himself to his limit.

SELECTIVE CURIOSITY

The entrepreneur, being goal oriented with respect to his work habits and directions of his business, is goal oriented with regard to his personal life. He recognizes that personal growth and development are synonymous with the growth of his business.

The man will constantly wish to grow as fast as his field. He consequently, continuously expands his intake of useful information. *"This tendency to probe, study and compare, to research, and to inquire into every phase of a given activity, is the one essential quality that separates the man from the dreamers in the quest for success, achievement, and great wealth."*[5] The growth orientation carries over to his personal habits. As with the information about his field, he is never satisfied with how far he, as a person, has developed. A person who steadily accepts new challenges, he searches for new and innovative ways to improve himself.

The entrepreneur has a field in which he cannot obtain enough information. The restaurateur eagerly learns everything about food and food service. The venture capitalist jumps at every opportunity to learn of why new businesses are successful. He "picks out" from the thousands of messages transmitted to him every day those which can help him and his business. These signals and clues may come from his markets, competitors, customers, suppliers, employees, or the news media. He absorbs more information about his industry and at a faster rate than the majority of people. He is constantly on the lookout for any "road signs" that may affect his business, even if a particular event does not seem to have direct significance.

As one might expect, when the president of a company combines a high degree of selective curiosity with a commitment to personal and business growth, the result is a constant atmosphere of change, not always for the better, in both the man and the organization. New products, policies, and production methods are the rule as opposed to the exception. Nothing is sacred; *change is the rule of the day.*

An entrepreneur, if caught in a mature company, will often find and in some cases, instigate conflict. When confronted with "superiors" in an organization, his desire for freedom, independence, and change often overrides his desire for acceptance on the part of his superiors. Formal procedures, continuing of the "old" ways are not for him, even though they may be the best course for a mature organization in a professional management stage. Entrepreneurs who wait until later in life to make their move will probably feature resumes with as many as five different organizations within ten years. *The job-hopping entrepreneur does so because he does not know that he is an entrepreneur. Once he realizes where he should be, he either makes his move or meshes personal goals with an organization he perceives will give him the needed experience and expertise to prepare him for his entrepreneurial adventure.*

COMPETITIVE/AGGRESSIVE

The entrepreneur is competitive. Not in the altruistic sense of competition with himself but rather he has *an intense need to compete with others.* To the entrepreneur, self-betterment is not an end but rather

a means of beating someone else. The marketplace is where the entrepreneur wants to compete. And once involved in a business of his
own, few outside competitive decisions make their way into his life.
However, during his youth, or while he is gaining experience in an organization, the need to fulfill his competitive urge in the marketplace
is not fulfilled. He will likely take up such diversions as sports or
games. Once a mastery of a sport or game is gained, he is likely to
move into another. This process may be repeated many times before
the man makes his move into the marketplace. As one might expect,
many of the sports are one-on-one as opposed to team (unless he is
the leader) or self-betterment. An entrepreneur would much rather
play poker than solitaire. Table 1 recapitulates those diversions an
entrepreneur will or will not engage in before he makes a move into
the marketplace.

TABLE 1. Pre-entrepreneurial Diversions.

Sport or Game	Highly Entrepreneurial	Perhaps Entrepreneurial	Not Entrepreneurial
Bridge		●	
Chess	●		
Fishing			●
Fencing	●		
Golf		●	
Handball	●		
Hunting			●
Ping Pong	●		
Squash	●		
Skiing			●
Surfing			●
Swimming			●
Baseball		●	
Basketball		●	
Football		●	
Hockey		●	
Tennis	●		
Racketball	●		
Fussball	●		
Skating			●
Bowling		●	
Track		●	

As was mentioned during the discussion on Maslow's application to the entrepreneur, once the entrepreneur has fulfilled his self-esteem needs, that is once he has surpassed a major milestone, an interest in self-improvement sports, such as skiing or golf, will appear. This is not true in the entrepreneur who has not yet passed a major milestone.

Right in line with competitiveness, the entrepreneur's strong ego drive and desire for self-esteem will most likely manifest itself in the form of undisguised aggressiveness. If the man is part of a larger organization, the aggressiveness will certainly alienate his peers, and eventually his immediate superiors.

He is sometimes called an "empire builder." With regard to rules and procedures, his attitude will be that they define what he cannot do. If not specifically restricted, he will assume the authority.

This aggressiveness is not only evident on the job, but also in the diversionary games in which he participates. "Winning is not the most important thing; it is the only thing." "If you don't play to win, why keep score?" Once in the marketplace, the aggressiveness pays off in the form of high profits and sales. The marketplace becomes the ideal outlet for the entrepreneur's overwhelming desire to dominate.

CREATIVITY

All people have some inherent creativity. Entrepreneurs, are they more creative than others? Unfortunately a direct answer to that question is not possible. There are many definitions of creativity. The one selected determines whether or not we call entrepreneurs creative. Since the relative merits of different definitions are beyond the scope of this book, only observations in this area will be mentioned.

We have previously observed that the entrepreneur is oriented toward innovation, improvement, and change. He has the ability to read others, and the environment — almost a clairvoyant ability to read the future and assess the risk. Similarly, being growth oriented, the entrepreneur is continuously seeking out new and different ways to expand his business faster or start a new one.

We have observed that one thing entrepreneurs do well is to associate, refine, and develop other's ideas into new and different ideas of their own. To demonstrate this point, all of us have read of very creative scientists who have developed revolutionary new processes or products only to fail in bringing them to the world. It took entre-

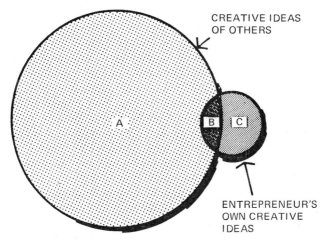

CREATIVE IDEAS
OF OTHERS

ENTREPRENEUR'S
OWN CREATIVE
IDEAS

FIGURE 25. Set of Creative Ideas.

preneurs to take this idea, massage it, combine it with other ideas and
then successfully go to market.

As this book is being written, we are seeing this very phenomena
develop. Dr. F. Wankel built the first rotary engine. Wankel formed
Wankel G.M.B.H. to develop and market the engine. This has been no
moneymaker. It took the relatively obscure Japanese firm of Fayo
Kogyo to develop and market it.

The above discussion is not designed to deny that the creative
individual scientist, for example, cannot be an entrepreneur. He can!
It is just that we see very few of them. Their existence may be explained as an intense ego drive and desire for independence. We can
also recognize an intermediate type entrepreneur. This entrepreneur
is one who is both creative in the scientific sense and can utilize both
his ideas and the ideas of others.

The franchise, a popular innovation of the latter part of the twen-
tieth century, has offered an excellent avenue for associative (Type A)
entrepreneurs, who, although they may have every other characteristic, need a vehicle to fulfill their objectives. The franchise is that
vehicle. Creative (Type C) entrepreneurs make very poor franchisees
and those that do enter the franchise chain either do things their
own way or get out in a hurry. Figure 25 illustrates the sets of
creative ideas and places the various types (A, B, and C) of entrepreneurs. Few Type C's enter the franchise market since by their
very nature they prefer to do things on their own. The combination,
that is the entrepreneur who can use other's ideas and create his own,
(Type B) on the other hand, proves both an asset and a liability

to the franchise industry. If the franchise is highly "prepackaged," a Type B will become bored and will probably not achieve the success of the Type A. Unfortunately, for many franchisors, they have overlooked the existence and problems inherent with both Type B's and Type C's. *As the franchisors become more sophisticated, they will concentrate their recruiting efforts on Type B's when the program is in its infancy and shift to Type A's as the program becomes highly "prepackaged."*

In conclusion, a list of nine personal traits that most entrepreneurs possess to one degree or another has been identified. Entrepreneurs are not unique in that many good leaders possess these traits as well. Similarly, some of them can be learned; other than intelligence and creativity, they are not inherited. The list does not include the admirable traits such as honesty, integrity, and regard for social and ecological good. Although most people will agree that people in a position of power and authority should possess the admirable traits, we have not found them necessary for entrepreneurial success. Of course, some entrepreneurs do possess them.

For those concerned with the apparent materialistic philosophy of entrepreneurs, one can take heart in an observation by Dr. Pat Moynihan, a special advisor to Presidents Kennedy and Johnson. He observed that as people and families rise on the social ladder, they become more conservative and less concerned with the social good. Only as outstanding success and wealth is achieved does social concern change. Frequently, the values of their offspring shift to a more liberal position. The Kennedys and Rockefellers are only two examples.

NOTES

[1] Wilson Learning Corporation, *Counselor Selling*, 1971, pages 16—20. The social style profile is but a small part of a process developed by the Wilson Learning Corporation in helping evaluate potential success. The authors recommend the use of the process (cost about $55.) for helping to determine the probability of entrepreneurial success. For more information, write to the Wilson Learning Corporation, 4900 Viking Drive, Minneapolis, Minnesota 55435.

[2] B. W. Bonnivier, "Managing Interpersonal Relationships," *Management Manual*, The Trane Company, 1972.

[3] University of Toronto, School of Business, Tapes "Seminar on Venture Capital," Time, Inc., 1972.

[4] John W. Atkinson, "Motivational Determinates of Risk Taking Behavior," *Psychological Review*, Vol. 64, No. 6, 1957, page 365.

[5] Howard L. Hill, *How to Think Like a Millionaire and Get Rich*, Prentice-Hall, Inc., 1968, p. 35.

6

ENTREPRENEURIAL BUSINESS OVERVIEW

The purposes of this chapter are twofold. The first is to briefly discuss the kinds of industries entrepreneurs most frequently enter and why. The second concern of this chapter is the entrepreneur's perspective toward his business, how he manages, and what kinds of control systems are used.

One way of approaching the question of why entrepreneurs are successful is to think in terms of what the entrepreneur does well. *All entrepreneurs and all businesses in general must do some things better than the competition. This can be called their critical capability.*

IBM's critical capability when it was a struggling new firm was research and development. In recent years, this has shifted more towards sales and customer service. One critical capability for General Motors, on the other hand, would be efficient production methods. For the outstanding corner meat market, it might be the butcher's ability to select the very best meat available from the local packinghouse.

Critical capabilities for entrepreneurs are many. They are not always a radical new product such as the Hula Hoop. In fact, most often entrepreneurial critical capabilities are such commonplace things as a new sales appeal, highly motivated salesmen, service or location, variety of products, quality, or cost. Many people associate entrepreneurs with Hula Hoop-type enterprises because of the romance and the visibility associated with this kind of business. It is the exception, however, rather than the rule.

To the entrepreneur, the concept or term of critical capability is usually foreign. He is asking questions such as, "What is it that I have to offer that will land the sales? Will my mousetrap entice customers from my competitors?" It should be pointed out that the previously discussed ability of many entrepreneurs to recombine and to rethink the new and innovative ideas of others is extremely important. It is from ideas of others that his ideas evolve which, in turn, eventually develop into critical capabilities.

In addition to a critical capability, the entrepreneur must do other things well. These can be broken down into Personnel, Technical or Product, and Business. That is not to say that one or more of these areas cannot be the critical capability. In fact, usually one or more of them is critical.

PEOPLE

Previous chapters have dealt at length with the entrepreneur's attitude toward his people. He has been pictured as an assertive and aggressive individual who is able to motivate his people to accomplish the seemingly impossible. Some of the tools in his bag include the high risk of failure environment and the high potential rewards if the business is successful.

In the terminology of Blake's management grid, the entrepreneur has been pictured as highly production oriented. With respect to people, entrepreneurs are found to range from high to low concern with the tendency toward the lower end. Having at least some concern for people plus the environment allows the entrepreneur to present to his employees a picture of himself as one who is colorful, and gregarious with a kind of charisma.

Successful entrepreneurs share a belief in the importance of supplementing their own talents with those of others. They know their limitations. Self-confident though they are, they don't regard themselves as gods. "The most important thing in business," says Neilson Harris, "is having people work with you, not for you."

The entrepreneur tends to surround himself, sometimes hesitatingly, with an "inner group" who satisfy the following two parameters. First, they are "in his image," that is, their personalities are similar, their attitudes are similar, and their values are similar. Second, they are not quite the type to do it on their own. They are entrepreneurial "doers" as opposed to entrepreneurial chief executives. Once this small, trustworthy corps is built, the rest of the organization reflects the group.

Even Lear, who has a reputation for being a lone wolf, emphasizes people. "The greatest mistake I ever made was hiring the second-best man for the job. You pay a terrible penalty for that. No matter what it costs, it's cheaper than hiring the second-best man."[1]

"The most important thing in any business," says Max Geffen (a magazine entrepreneur worth about $50,000,000) "is attaching the right people to you. The people below you. The people next to you and the people above you."[2]

"One thing I try to do is regard my executives as partners. My father used to tell me, 'Son, don't worry about how much money you're going to make. Get the right guy in and make him a lot of money and that's all you'll need.' I've always followed that advise."[3]

With the exception noted in Chapter 1, ideally the entrepreneur would be able to delegate decision making to the man or department closely associated with the responsibility of accomplishing the objective. If he does have one major fault, this must be it. The entrepreneur does not delegate well. He may communicate his objectives and, even if a theory X man, change and modify the objectives according to input from his "inner group," but he does not delegate well. He may assign the "what," and the "when," but he also tries to decide the "how to." At the slightest provocation, he will intrude in the midst of the task to take personal control over the situation, only to relinquish the reins a few days later and wonder why the task was not completed on schedule. He will follow very loose lines of communication and authority. Every subordinate is expected to be able to handle everything and, if the subordinates, the entrepreneur, and the organization last long enough, almost everyone will have accomplished something in marketing, finance, manufacturing, and management.

PRODUCT OR SERVICE

The entrepreneur, by definition, faces restrictions that are more demanding than those for a mature business. Two such restrictions largely determine the types of businesses entrepreneurs start and the more mundane aspects of their management. These restrictions are (1) limited initial capital resources and (2) high degrees of uncertainty with respect to success.

Sources of new venture capital have mushroomed in recent years. Today's entrepreneur usually does not face serious problems in securing necessary capital to start his business. The problem he does face, however, is that as more and more outside funds are acquired, he loses more and more control of his business. This, of course, is an untenable position for the entrepreneur. He wants absolute control. He must therefore consider capital as limited.

Because of these restrictions placed on the entrepreneur, his product or service is usually characterized by the following criteria:[4]

- The products or service is of a low fixed cost — low breakeven nature. That is, a relatively small amount must be invested in fixed-cost items such as land, buildings, or machines. Most costs will be of the variable type that vary with the level of production such as direct labor and direct materials. A low break-even firm is one that does not require a large sales volume to recover all costs.

- The product is nonperishable.

- The product does not require special or unusual handling.

- The product is quick-turn. That is, once the product is finished being manufactured, it does not require a long period of time before it is bought by a consumer. The product or service may even be "made to order," thus requiring an absolute minimum of time as finished inventory (hours or at most a few days).

- The product does not require much time to produce.

- The product or service does not require a large expenditure in research and development.

- Unless it has either an extremely low break even or the entrepreneur and his inner group are technological leaders in the field, the entrepreneur will not go into a business that has a high degree of technological obsolescence.

- Few entrepreneurs enter the marketplace with a product or service that is not essential or that does not fit in with the overall market the way it is at the present moment.

- Orders for the product or service are not too small.

- The entrepreneur may start by being a subcontractor for a few or even one account, since this reduces advertising and marketing expenditures to a minimum, but he soon attracts more customers or diversifies his line so that his business is not entirely dependent on a few accounts.

- The product will tend to have small production runs, thus the manufacturing facilities tend to be flexible.

- If the product or service is nearly the same as some well-entrenched competitors, the entrepreneur will have found a way to produce it for less. On the other hand, the product or service may be so unique that production methods may not be of major consequence in the early stages of the business.

- Legal problems are minimal.

- Extensive credit is not required.

- Labor as a percent of sales is not excessive. Non-union labor can be used.

Unless the entrepreneur is willing to give up a substantial amount of equity, his product or service will be limited.

Not only are the industries or types of businesses somewhat restricted but the environment imposes certain restrictions on the entrepreneur's outlook and actions. Most of these have been discussed previously but warrant additional comment. Due to the selective curiosity or thirst for knowledge of the entrepreneur, he keeps abreast of his product and industry as well as any new investment opportunities. He probably subscribes to any journals or periodicals pertinent to his product, probably knows a few of the "big names" in the industry on a personal basis, and probably instilled the same "thirst" for industry knowledge in his inner group. Conversations with acquaintances concern his business, product or industry as opposed to golf, fishing, the children or world affairs. Here we have a man who dislikes detail, but plows through whatever he can find that will increase his knowledge and therefore increase his success.

If the product or service involves a high level of technology in either the manufacture or sales, the entrepreneur knows the technical aspects. He may not personally know it all, but the people he has hired will! Once committed, the entrepreneur cannot survive if the production process or technical applications do not perform as predicted.

BUSINESS MANAGEMENT

The prime entrepreneurial goals are GROWTH and PROFIT. Toward this end, the entrepreneur has assembled an outstanding team and has researched the product and process. These activities alone, however, do not insure growth and profit. The business management function still remains. This is the key domain of the entrepreneur!

To digress for a moment, many are critical of the profit goal in our contemporary society. To the entrepreneur, however, profit must remain of primary importance. To the entrepreneur, profit is the only measure of success available. Profit is the only way he can measure accomplishments or movement toward self-fulfillment. In addition, profit provides that all important track record — the so-called "proof of the pudding" which the entrepreneur must have in order to secure low-cost funds for future expansion.

Within the mind of the entrepreneur, a goal of high growth and profit is too vague to serve as an operating guide. The goals are thus broken down into three sub-goals. These are:

1. Maximizing and meshing sales and production volume

2. Controlling all costs

3. Maintaining an adequate cash position.

Figure 26 shows how the entrepreneur views the relationship between personnel, technical, and business management functions and the profit goal. It also shows the relationship between the three sub-goals; i.e., sales and production volume, cash position, and cost control to the business management function. To the skilled entrepreneur, realistic concrete goals can be established.

Techniques used to achieve these sub-goals and the importance of each varies between firms. To some, they will represent critical capabilities, to others some parts will be of lesser importance. For example, direct costs in a small retail establishment are of minimal concern. Direct costs in a manufacturing concern are extremely important.

The remainder of this chapter is devoted to describing the entrepreneur's attitude toward and approaches to these goals. The approaches are in very rudimentary form. Entrepreneurs with a business education use more sophisticated tools — these represent the bare minimum. The reader should recall that the authors are reporting what is, not what should be.

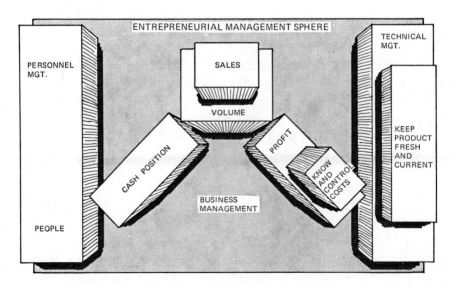

FIGURE 26. Entrepreneurial Management Sphere.

It is easy to criticize anyone in charge of anything unless one has been there himself. The entrepreneurial mind, just as the mind of any person in a position of responsibility, seldom has the opportunity to "fine tune" his thought processes. We should not be critical of the fact that there seem to be some incongruities in the way his business puzzle is put together, but delighted that it is put together in as meaningful a pattern as it is.

SALES AND PRODUCTION VOLUME

"A business with no business is no business." No entrepreneur ever lost sight of this fact. It is surprising that many large corporations, those in the latter part of the professional management stage or in the early part of the obsolescent management stage, lose sight of sales as a critical part of their business.

Reference is made to Figure 27, which shows the relationships between the goals and accounting procedures.

Initially, the entrepreneur's enthusiasm will provide the necessary sales, as he will be doing the selling. As any professional salesman realizes, once one is convinced of his product and thoroughly understands it, he is well on the way to making a sale. Combine a basic belief that his product is superior, a thorough understanding of the product, an inner need to succeed, and a high empathic ability, and you have a salesman. And, you have sales. At this stage in his business development he will use the small size of his organization as a selling tool, explaining to customers that he must "give a better job" to use as an example to other potential customers, or that the small firm will be flexible enough to meet the customer's changing needs. Since he makes sales easily, he has a tendency to oversimplify: "If we need more sales, we'll just add salesmen."

Very seldom will any entrepreneur make a sale or allow a sale to be made at or below cost. He takes such negotiation as a personal insult, since the product is not just his, it is him. Only in rare cases, to "get in bed" with a potentially heavy customer, will he allow such a practice, and only when the customer understands fully that it is just a one-time order to prove to the customer that the entrepreneur's product is superior or his service better.

If a sales decline is imminent, the entrepreneur will, except in the most extraordinary circumstances, increase his sales and promotional activities. His solution to an imminent sales decline is not to cut back inventories, production runs, or people, but to "do whatever it takes

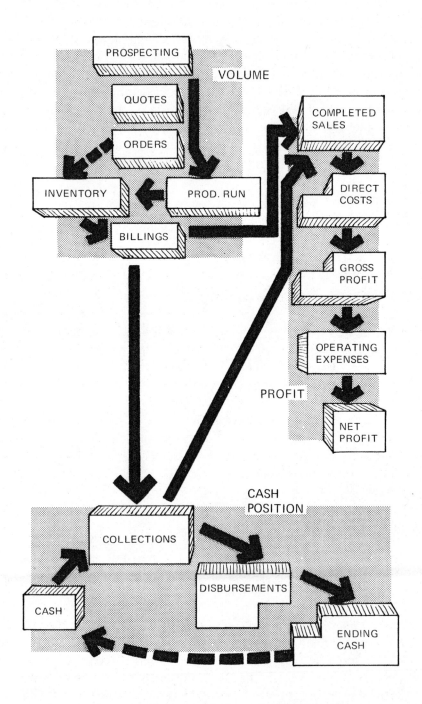

FIGURE 27. Entrepreneurial Perception of Profit.

to get profitable sales in the door." In extraordinary circumstances, such as a competitive product that makes an entrepreneur's product obsolete, he will ruthlessly reorganize, restructure, perhaps fire many of his people in order to keep his business profitable and surviving.

VOLUME

Volume is both production volume and sales volume. The higher the prospecting, the higher the profit, assuming, of course, the rest of the lines operate the same way at any volume. Prospecting is simply going out and looking for those who might have a need for the product. Suppose we have a service that can be used to help small businesses collect overdue bills. Prospecting for a particular city might be:

1. Going to the Chamber of Commerce and obtaining a list of all companies with 100 or less employees. Subjectively going down the list and crossing off those who would not have a need for the service. Then completing the prospecting by contacting the potential customer with:

    a. A personal visit

    b. A phone call

    c. A direct mail piece.

2. Indirect prospecting can be accomplished via advertising in the newspaper, billboard, television, or radio.

The entrepreneur will keep track of his rate of lead generation. The definition of a lead is "someone who is interested." This lead generation information will probably be expressed in terms of cost per lead and also leads per category — person per period of time. (Or leads per category per period of time if there is not a direct correlation between people and leads — newspaper advertising would be an example.) For example, say we have two telephone solicitors prospecting for our collection service. For the past three weeks, these girls have produced 200 names of businesses who are interested. Assuming that each girl is paid $50/week and that out-of-pocket costs for two phones for three weeks were $100, the cost per lead would be calculated as follows:

$$\text{Cost per lead} = \frac{\text{Dollars expended during the period}}{\text{Number of leads obtained during the period}} =$$

$$\frac{(50 \times 2)3 + 100}{200} = \$2.00 \text{ per lead.}$$

Leads per category — person per period of time is calculated as follows:

$$\begin{array}{l}\text{Leads per category —} \\ \text{person per period} \\ \text{of time}\end{array} = \frac{\text{Leads by category}}{(\text{No. of people in category}) \, (\text{time period})}$$

$$\frac{200}{(2)(3)} = 33 \text{ leads per telephone girl per week.}$$

With such information the entrepreneur would allocate $924.00 per week for lead-generating activities and hire 12 more girls if he wanted to obtain 462 leads a week.

Once those who might have a need for the product or service are identified, the entrepreneur goes out of his way to make a "quote." A quote is a specific attempt to obtain a specific amount of business. A quote rate, or quotes per lead will be kept to obtain a feel for the quality of the leads as well as for estimating his lead cost per sale. If a salesman had been given 300 leads and submitted 100 quotes, the quote rate would be 33%.

A closure rate, by salesman and for the entrepreneur will be roughly kept. Thus, a salesman who had given 100 quotes and who comes back with 60 orders would have a 60% closure rate. In some cases it will be impossible to distinguish between a quote and a lead. In such cases only a lead rate would be kept, and the assumption would be made that a quote is a lead. This closure rate may have to be more subjective than quantifiable. In the example above, it is relatively simple and it does not take into account any "closeable quotes outstanding" (those leads that have turned into quotes but for which the salesman has not received a definite "yes" or "no"). The closure rate may have to be extremely subjective when one is calling upon industrial prospects, or other accounts whose business takes a great deal of relationship building before any business is obtained.

Once the quote is closed, it then becomes an order. The amount of orders the entrepreneur and his salesmen obtain in a period of time will be kept. With the order well in hand, the entrepreneur either obtains the product from finished goods inventory, or more likely, he gears up his production to meet the order demand. Obviously, he does not accept an order that is too far above his capacity, but exactly what his capacity is and exactly what is too far above it are parameters that are not clearly defined, not even to the entrepreneur himself. He will take or reject the order based upon his "gut feel" of his absolute maximum production capacity. If he has salesmen working for him, their quotas will be based on the same type of "gut feel." As the business grows beyond the one-man stage, he will probably develop a very simple way to measure production capacity. In a job-shop[5] type manufacturing endeavor, this measure of capacity might be $ output/production man/week. This may be true even if he had diverse products selling at varying levels. For example, if his past three months' sales were $650,000 and he had an average of 10 production people working for him, he would quickly calculate that his production capacity is as shown below:

$$\frac{\text{Sales During The Period}}{(\text{Weeks in the period})(\text{Number of production men in the period})} =$$

$$\text{\$ Output/production man/week}$$

$$\frac{650,000}{(13)(10)} = \text{\$5,000/production man/week.}$$

On the other hand, in a production-line operation, where machines, not people, are rate determining, his approach is different. Output per operating hour becomes the critical measure of capacity. For example, if sales for a 10-week period were $320,000 and no overtime was used, the entrepreneur measures production capacity as follows:

$$\frac{\text{Total Output in \$}}{\text{Time converted to hours}} = \text{Output per hour}$$

$$\frac{\$320,000}{(10 \times 5 \times 8)} = \text{\$800. per hour.}$$

The time period must be long enough to cover maintenance time, down-time, change-over time, and recovery rate; that is, all disruptions to production.

Accordingly he would attempt to sell, or have his salesmen sell, at least the weekly production capacity, but might accept orders higher than that figure, but not too much higher. The rule of thumb and the method of arriving at it may vary from entrepreneur to entrepreneur, but he will have a handle, albeit not exact, on his production capacity.

His production scheduling would probably consist of giving the order to the production supervisor and saying he should get it done by such and such a date.

If the product or service violates the criterion of minimal time to produce previously discussed, the entrepreneur will advance bill the customer as the production run is in process or as the service is being completed. More than likely the billing will go out as soon as the product or service is complete, but never too long after.

The following information is then available for an entrepreneurial management decision:

1. The cost per lead and leads per category per period of time

2. The quote rate per lead

3. A closure rate per quote

4. An order rate per salesman per period of time

5. Production capacity.

Taking these figures, even in very rough form and even not extremely accurate, some very major decisions may be made. If we double our sales force, how many more production men will we need? If the men are now working with 100% efficiency (subjective input), naturally we double the production force. If our production line is expanded from one to two shifts, how must the sales policy be changed and the sales force increased? Are the manufacturing facilities adequate to handle a doubling in volume? Subjectively he assures himself that they will be or guesses how much out-of-pocket money it will take to gear them up. How many more salesmen should we add? How much money should we allocate to lead generating activities? What happens if we add 10 salesmen? And so on.

Probably the reader has just asked himself, "Where will the entrepreneur get the money to gear up for higher production, especially if he adds 10 salesmen?" This brings us to our next entrepreneurial goal — cash position. Looking back at Figure 27 we see that cash position is a function of:

1. Beginning cash

2. The rate of collections (or the rate of billings)

3. The rate of disbursements.

Armed with the above three pieces of information, the entrepreneur can see what the limit is — cashwise — on his business. Beginning cash is easy enough to obtain. The rate of collections is really a result of his credit policy; even if we assume the completed-contract method of accounting,[6] the collection rate is usually expressed as some function of sales. For example, the entrepreneur might determine that collections during a month are roughly equal to the sales during the previous month, that is, his accounts receivable days = 30. A restaurant would probably have accounts receivable days = 0, that is, all cash sales (collections would equal sales in this case). The disbursement rate is also a function of sales, both the previous month's and the current month's. Some expenses can be disbursed in the future (accounts payable days) while some costs are disbursed immediately (payroll for example). Suppose that the entrepreneur has determined that disbursements during a month equal 30% of this month's sales and 60% of previous month's sales. This mix will become apparent to the entrepreneur, even if he does not keep accurate accounting records, because he will probably be writing the checks and will have a good "gut feel" of what goes out when.

Recapitulating then:

1. Beginning cash is obtained from the checkbook.

2. Collections for a month are obtained from the collection rate, which will be a function of sales (previous month's and possibly current month's).

3. Disbursements for a month are obtained from a disbursement rate, which will be a function of sales (this month's plus possibly the previous month's).

4. Ending cash, or cash available for expansion purposes can easily be calculated by the difference in the collection and disbursement rates.

The entrepreneur may not have a firm grasp of working capital, or even go through a pencil and paper calculation of cash available for expansion purposes, but he intuitively will go through the above four steps when making a decision involving a cash outlay. If his guestimates prove faulty, and he runs out of money, he will increase his rate of collections, increase his accounts payable, or in extreme cases, borrow. Surprisingly enough, cash is not often a problem for the entrepreneur. It is even accurate to state that *an entrepreneurial adventure rarely will fail due to lack of funds.* If it goes "belly up," money is not the reason. Many businesses are started with no ($0) capital. A resourceful entrepreneur can figure out ways to get by without money.

The subject of cash in a business deserves another comment. Too much cash available can be disastrous. *Cash makes you careless. Just as work is spent to fill the time available, so cash is spent if it is available.* Business discipline demands that cash be spent wisely, especially if it is someone else's (other stockholders' or a bank's). Too much of a bank loan released too soon, overcapitalization via a large stock issue, are not proper crutches for the entrepreneur. The battle for survival must be waged on a tight cash flow.

COST CONTROL – PROFIT

The controlling of costs, setting prices and determining profit are so interdependent that it is not possible to discuss them separately. The starting point is sales. From sales is deducted all the direct costs associated with the product or service. Direct costs include labor required to make the product, the raw materials that went into the product, any subcontractor costs, any sales commissions paid for the particular product, and anything else that can be directly attributable to a particular job. The entrepreneur will manage by exception. The biggest variance in direct cost will probably occur in labor. The entrepreneur will have estimated in his own mind, or have calculated from past experience, what his labor as a percent of sales should be.

On as infrequently as a monthly basis, he will total up his payroll, divide that by sales for the month, and use that piece of information to gauge his cost control. This, of course, does not take into account any "unapplied labor," that is that labor expended on things that cannot be charged to a sale, such as painting the truck, cleaning up the shop, or building a storage rack. *This management, by exception, is not 100% accurate; it is not acceptable by academic or professional standards, but it is quick and works well enough by entrepreneurial standards.* If an entrepreneur spots a serious variance, say in labor as discussed above, he takes *immediate* action. It is not surprising to see him run to the production area and start a discussion with the production men without the production supervisor anywhere in sight. He may fire someone on the spot; he may call the situation to everyone's attention and let them know what has to be done right now; he may do anything, but he will not hesitate to do something. This is his method of controlling costs.

There is another course of action that the entrepreneur keeps in his bag of tricks. *He may just raise prices,* or keep prices high enough to cover all possible cost overruns that could occur. The business probably is producing something unique in the marketplace and severe competition has not yet entered, so the entrepreneur just keeps raising prices until people stop buying.

Sales minus direct costs equals gross profit. The entrepreneur will most likely use a relatively simple accounting system to obtain all of his direct costs or may use a quick and dirty way of obtaining direct costs similar to that discussed for labor above. In any event, he will obtain, on a monthly basis, at least a very rough idea of his gross margins. He will look at gross margins as a percent of sales. If the gross margins are lower than anticipated, and his labor as a percent of sales is within estimates, this lets him know that either his selling price is too low, or one of his other direct costs is out of line. Thus he uses his gross margin (expressed as a percent of sales) as a method of control.

Gross margin less operating expenses equals profit before taxes. Operating expenses are all those expense items that cannot be directly attributed to a job (salaries, office space, land, trucks, and the like).

The entrepreneur has a vague idea what overhead should run during a month and intuitively holds all the overhead down to a minimum. Used furniture, leased equipment, low rent offices are commonplace during the entrepreneurial management stage. Via a relatively simple accounting system, the entrepreneur is able to keep a ballpark estimate of overhead.

Net profit before taxes is the result. An accounting system is not the only way the entrepreneur can tell if he is losing money. If he is and has no accounting system, he will know in a hurry — his bank account will run out. The danger, however, is that he may not be losing money. The bank account can run out just as rapidly if accounts receivable or inventory is increasing. During the business start-up phases the entrepreneur will sometimes not bother implementing a paperwork system which yields the accounting data, but not long after the first sale is completed he will have seen the necessity and, although reluctantly, implement some sort of accounting procedures. From the profit portion we have the following information.

1. Net profit before taxes

2. Overhead or operating expenses

3. Gross margin as a percent of sales

4. Any highly variable portions of direct cost, expressed as a percent of sales

Recapitulating the entire entrepreneurial business-management process, he obtains little more than the following information.

1. *The cost per lead and leads per category per period of time*

2. *The quote rate per lead*

3. *The closure rate per quote*

4. *The order rate per man*

5. *Production capacity*

6. *Beginning cash*

7. *The collection rate*

8. *The disbursement rate*

9. *Gross margin as a percent of sales*

10. *Any highly variable portion of direct cost, as a percent of sales*

11. *Overhead*

12. *Net profit before taxes*

With these pieces of information, the entrepreneur can manage his business, even though it is not in a sophisticated manner, even though there may be a lot of "slop" in the system. We are reminded again of Druckers' statement "Maximization of opportunities is a . . .

precise definition of the entrepreneurial job. It implies that effectiveness rather than efficiency is essential in business. The pertinent question is not how to do things right but how to find the right things to do, and to concentrate resources and efforts on them."

In conclusion, it is necessary to place this rudimentary accounting system in perspective. It is neither accurate, sophisticated, nor acceptable for more mature companies. For an entrepreneur, however, it does represent the bare minimum necessary for decision-making purposes. More learned and sophisticated entrepreneurs will incorporate for more advanced techniques in operating their business.

NOTES

[1] "The Incurables," *Forbes,* July 1, 1969, page 21.

[2] *Ibid.*

[3] *Ibid.* page 21.

[4] For a more detailed description of many of the criteria mentioned in this chapter, see Louis A. Allen, *Starting and Succeeding In Your Own Small Business,* Grosset & Dunlop, Inc., 1968.

[5] Job-shop production — Operation in which each employee works on a project from beginning to end. For example, an automobile repair shop. This is as opposed to a continuous production line.

[6] With the completed-contract method of accounting, a sale is defined as a sale only after the job is complete and the final billing is made.

7

THE
BUSINESS
START-UP

Since the entrepreneur is so vitally concerned with the start-up of his business, the authors deemed it appropriate to include this chapter which delineates a normative model for the start-up of a profit-making organization. Some of the 57 steps shown are for that of a manufacturing concern. However, those steps concerned solely with manufacturing concerns may be deleted for other types of start-ups. For those entrepreneurs ready to make their move, the addition of a horizontal time axis as well as fixing of responsibility to a person for each event is recommended.

OBJECTIVE OF THE MODEL

The objective of the business start-up is to form a road map of sequential steps that will insure that a logical thought process has been followed with the minimum amount of dollar outlay.

The model will start with the very "incubation period" right through until the business is a going concern. The model is broken down into three basic components: The Concept, The Plan, and The Implementation. Figure 28, the network diagram of the complete business start-up model, shows the various components as well as sub-components of the model. Each basic phase, that is The Concept, The Plan, and The Implementation is broken down into sub-milestones. The objective of each phase as well as each sub-milestone will be stated along with some supplementary comments by the authors concerning the most important factors which should be considered.

THE CONCEPT

Objective: The objective of the concept phase is to evaluate both the entrepreneur and the potential business idea with the minimum of dollar outlay.

I. THE CONCEPT

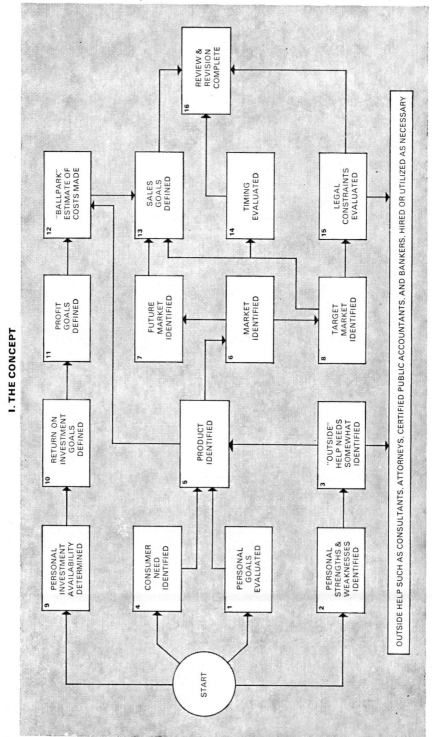

OUTSIDE HELP SUCH AS CONSULTANTS, ATTORNEYS, CERTIFIED PUBLIC ACCOUNTANTS, AND BANKERS, HIRED OR UTILIZED AS NECESSARY

II. THE PLAN

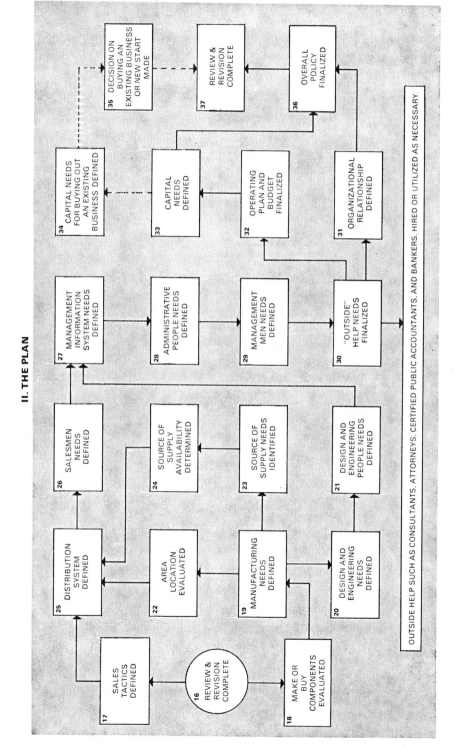

OUTSIDE HELP SUCH AS CONSULTANTS, ATTORNEYS, CERTIFIED PUBLIC ACCOUNTANTS, AND BANKERS, HIRED OR UTILIZED AS NECESSARY.

16 REVIEW & REVISION COMPLETE

17 SALES TACTICS DEFINED

18 MAKE OR BUY COMPONENTS EVALUATED

19 MANUFACTURING NEEDS DEFINED

20 DESIGN AND ENGINEERING NEEDS DEFINED

21 DESIGN AND ENGINEERING PEOPLE NEEDS DEFINED

22 AREA LOCATION EVALUATED

23 SOURCE OF SUPPLY NEEDS IDENTIFIED

24 SOURCE OF SUPPLY AVAILABILITY DETERMINED

25 DISTRIBUTION SYSTEM DEFINED

26 SALESMEN NEEDS DEFINED

27 MANAGEMENT INFORMATION SYSTEM NEEDS DEFINED

28 ADMINISTRATIVE PEOPLE NEEDS DEFINED

29 MANAGEMENT MEN NEEDS DEFINED

30 "OUTSIDE" HELP NEEDS FINALIZED

31 ORGANIZATIONAL RELATIONSHIP DEFINED

32 OPERATING PLAN AND BUDGET FINALIZED

33 CAPITAL NEEDS DEFINED

34 CAPITAL NEEDS FOR BUYING OUT AN EXISTING BUSINESS DEFINED

35 DECISION ON BUYING AN EXISTING BUSINESS OR NEW START MADE

36 OVERALL POLICY FINALIZED

37 REVIEW & REVISION COMPLETE

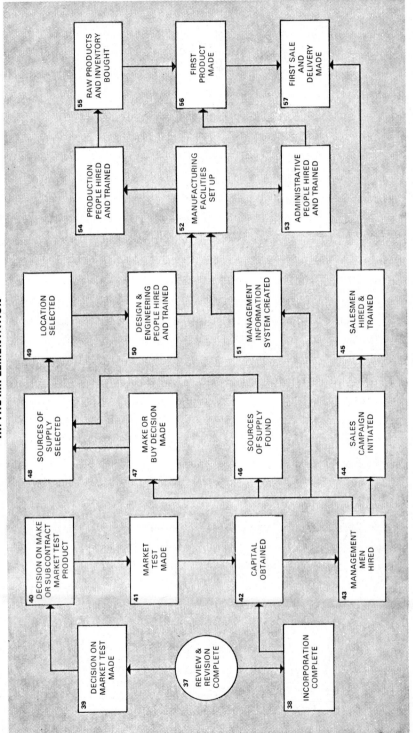

III. THE IMPLEMENTATION

39 DECISION ON MARKET TEST MADE

37 REVIEW & REVISION COMPLETE

38 INCORPORATION COMPLETE

40 DECISION ON MAKE OR SUBCONTRACT MARKET TEST PRODUCT

41 MARKET TEST MADE

42 CAPITAL OBTAINED

43 MANAGEMENT MEN HIRED

44 SALES CAMPAIGN INITIATED

45 SALESMEN HIRED & TRAINED

46 SOURCES OF SUPPLY FOUND

47 MAKE OR BUY DECISION MADE

48 SOURCES OF SUPPLY SELECTED

49 LOCATION SELECTED

50 DESIGN & ENGINEERING PEOPLE HIRED AND TRAINED

51 MANAGEMENT INFORMATION SYSTEM CREATED

52 MANUFACTURING FACILITIES SET UP

53 ADMINISTRATIVE PEOPLE HIRED AND TRAINED

54 PRODUCTION PEOPLE HIRED AND TRAINED

55 RAW PRODUCTS AND INVENTORY BOUGHT

56 FIRST PRODUCT MADE

57 FIRST SALE AND DELIVERY MADE

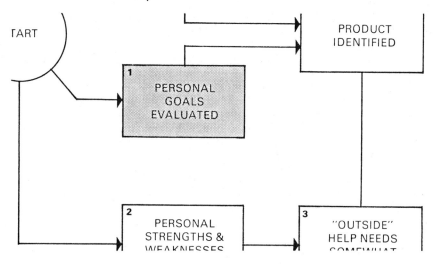

OBJECTIVE: Clearly Identify the Personal Goals of the Entrepreneur.

This is one of the most obvious, yet one of the least completed steps in most business start-ups. The president's personal goals must be expressed in terms of money. As was explained previously, money is not the end in itself but just the way that the entrepreneur keeps score. *Unless his goals are stated in monetary terms, the success of the venture is dubious at best.* Personal goals such as prestige, being at a certain place in life at a certain period of time, family happiness, or any degree of self-actualization are not proper personal goals for the first-time entrepreneur.

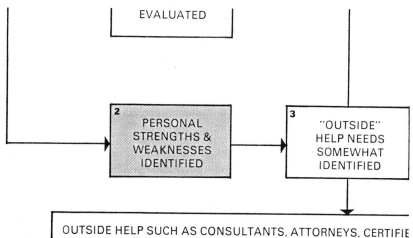

OBJECTIVE: Complete a Personal Balance Sheet of Both Assets and Liabilities of the Entrepreneur.

Personal characteristics, psychological characteristics, background, *ability to handle cash wisely* and physical stamina must be taken into account. Perhaps the best basis for determining the entrepreneur's strengths and weaknesses is to compare him with the profile presented in this book. As was mentioned at the start of the book, every entrepreneur need not possess every characteristic mentioned, but a reasonable degree of correlation should be expected, or else the business is doomed to a failure no matter how excellent the marketing idea. One distinct advantage of this balance sheet is that it will immediately show in what areas the potential entrepreneur is weak and in what areas he must staff his organization in order to overcome these weaknesses.

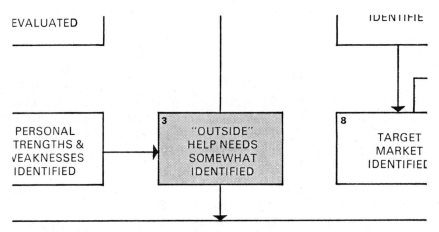

ᵖ SUCH AS CONSULTANTS, ATTORNEYS, CERTIFIED PUBLIC ACCOUNTANTS

OBJECTIVE: Identify Those Areas Which the Entrepreneur Will Have to Go to Outside His Organization in Order to Insure a Successful Business Start-Up.

From the previous milestone, one should be able to immediately identify those particular areas which are outside the entrepreneur's expertise, as well as those areas he will probably staff internally in the organization. For example, consultants, attorneys, certified public accountants, and certain banking expertise may be required. From the balance sheet it should be clear in which areas the entrepreneur does not possess expertise. Therefore, a tentative list of outside needs can be identified.

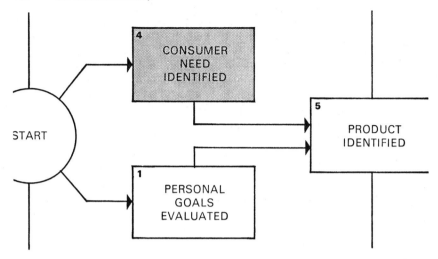

OBJECTIVE: Identify the Consumer Need or Needs Which Will Form the Basis of the Business.

As with a previously discussed milestone, this is an obvious step, yet many businessmen fail to really consider this step in depth. One must insure that a proper consumer need exists both for the short and near term before a venture is started. At this point in the start-up model *one should not consider the competition as it exists today in a particular industry.*

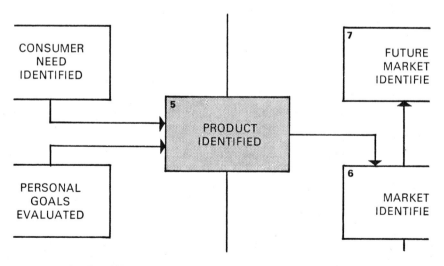

OBJECTIVE: Solidly Identify the Product with Which the Business Will Concern Itself.

Once the consumer need has been identified, the product itself may or may not be readily visible. The identification of the product step is one which should require a great deal of "brainstorming" and should attempt to minimize personal prejudices and knowledge about a particular industry. Many fascinating and unusual products have resulted from complete free thinking during this step. When this milestone is complete, the product and all of its specifications should be identified both in the entrepreneur's mind and on paper.

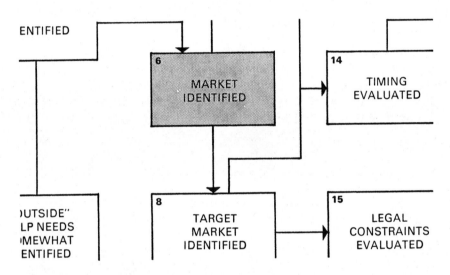

OBJECTIVE: Insure that the Overall Market for a Product Is Quantitatively Identified.

Once the entrepreneur has the product clearly in mind, he must insure that a sufficient market exists for his product. Markets themselves are usually a function of population and the traditional identification of market process is a study of characteristics and trends of people. One must insure that the market is large enough in order to sustain not just an embryonic business but also a very large, hopefully multi-million dollar organization.

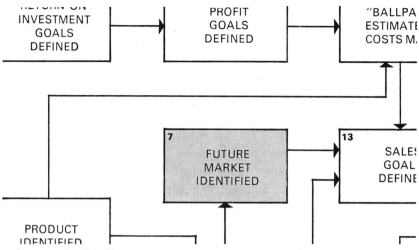

OBJECTIVE: Identify the Market for the Product as It Will Exist
in Three to Five Years in the Future.

A mere extrapolation of the past trends is not sufficient in to-day's extremely fast-changing world. For example, from past statistics it would appear that the world dog population would be double the number in the year 2000 as it was in the year 1970. An entrepreneur might create a new type of dog food to fulfill this potential market. With such an extreme increase in the number of canines there would obviously be a tremendous future market for this type of product. Or would it? In the year 2000 will the population of dogs have doubled? It is quite within the realm of possibility that within the United States there will be no domestic pets alive at that period in time. The point is with the extremely rapid changing marketplace, one must gaze into his crystal ball at length before he makes an investment of his time and money.

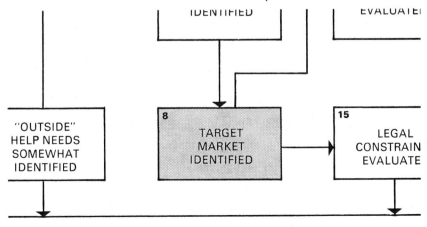

OBJECTIVE: Pinpoint the Specific Area or Segment of the Market
that the Entrepreneur Will Attack.

Target markets should be something that the entrepreneur can "hold in his hand." He must be able to clearly see and identify all of the characteristics within the particular segment of the market which he is preparing to penetrate. The identification of the target market should be in extreme detail and much more precise than the identification of the overall market. As part of the detailed analysis, an estimate of the per unit selling price is in order.

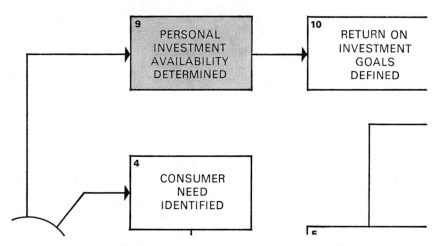

OBJECTIVE: Quantitatively Evaluate the Entrepreneur's Potential Equity in His Business.

A complete personal balance sheet should be taken in order that the entrepreneur can evaluate exactly how much equity he will be able to put into the business. The amount of equity will obviously be much less than his personal net worth; however, his personal net worth can be utilized as security for debt.

I. THE CONCEPT

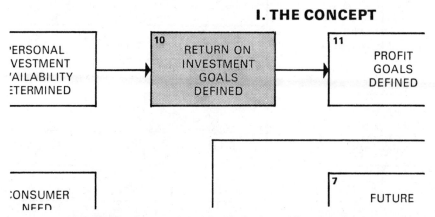

OBJECTIVE: Quantitatively Identify the Annual Return on Investment the Entrepreneur Must Make.

The annual rate of return should obviously be expressed in terms of percentage. If the entrepreneur's equity is $50,000, and he wishes to double that every year or double that the first year, his return on investment goal would be 100% per year. Returns of 50% to 1000% per year are not uncommon for entrepreneurs.

I. THE CONCEPT

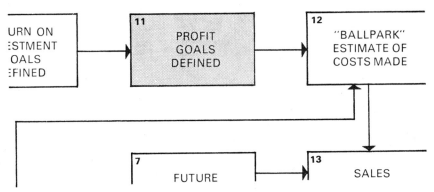

OBJECTIVE: Quantitatively Identify the Profit that the Entrepreneur Must Make in Order to Satisfy His Return on Investment Goals.

With the equity identified as well as the return on investment goals expressed in terms of an annual percentage rate clearly identified, the defining of the profit goals is relatively simple. For example, if the entrepreneur has an initial equity investment of $50,000 and his return on investment goals per year are 100%, he must make $50,000 profit the first year (assuming he is the sole stockholder), $100,000 profit the second year, $200,000 profit the third year, $400,000 profit the fourth year and so on.

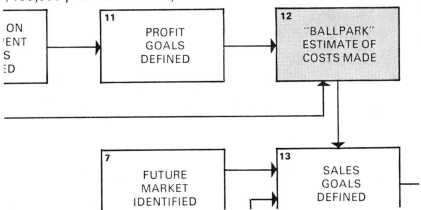

OBJECTIVE: Make a Reasonable Estimate on the Costs Involved to Produce the Product or Service Required.

Industry standards are the best method for determining costs. If no present industry exists, either a consultant or one familiar with the process the product will have to go through in order to be created will have to be utilized. Costs include not only direct costs (those costs associated directly with the manufacturer of the item) but also overhead costs.

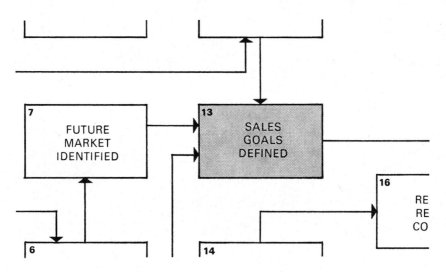

OBJECTIVE: Quantitatively Identify Those Sales Goals Which the Entrepreneur Must Meet, and Develop a Succinct Marketing Strategy.

With the profit goals defined and the ballpark estimate of costs made, the identification of sales goals is simple. Sales minus costs equals profit. In reverse, profit plus costs equal sales goals. The sales goals should be expressed monthly for the first year and yearly for the next three to four years thereafter.

The reader should note the manner in which the sales goals were defined. *Sales goals are a function of profit goals; profit goals are a function of return on investment goals.* Unfortunately many new businesses do not follow this approach. Instead they set sales goals and calculate how much they will make. This latter manner, although very common, is incorrect. *One must decide what he must make and then determine his sales goals.*

A concise marketing strategy must be developed, usually less than fifty words in length. *It states what is to be done, not how to do it.*

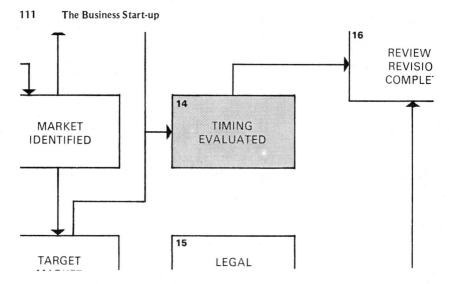

OBJECTIVE: Insure that the Business Is Being Started Off at a Time Which Is Not Severely Detrimental to the Success of the Business.

A good entrepreneur can make almost any business go at almost any time. Almost is the word to note in the previous sentence. One should insure that the industry, the market, or the nation as a whole is not heading into a severe depression. Very few entrepreneurs, no matter how good they personally were, have weathered a severe depression in the demand for their product or service during the start-up period. If the outlook is either up or neutral, then the timing is appropriate.

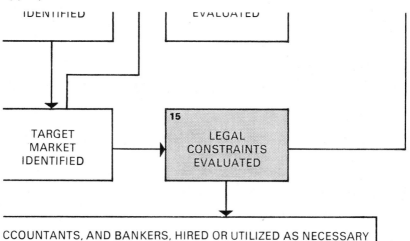

OBJECTIVE: Insure that Any and All Legal Constraints Are Identified and Evaluated.

As the United States becomes more and more affluent, the number of laws on the books of the United States increases geometrically. These laws may take various forms and may seem complex and burdensome to the small businessman. If this is the way it appears to the small businessman, it is because it is true. One cannot hope to comply with each and every specific law and potential legal crossover that could be made; however, a reasonable identification of the legal constraints must be made by a competent attorney. Just because it appears that a particular point "might be illegal," the entrepreneur should not abandon his plans. *When a business is small, it can do almost anything, and at times has to do almost anything, in order to survive.* As long as the risks are known, the entrepreneur can make a decision on whether or not he wishes to encroach upon any legal guidelines.

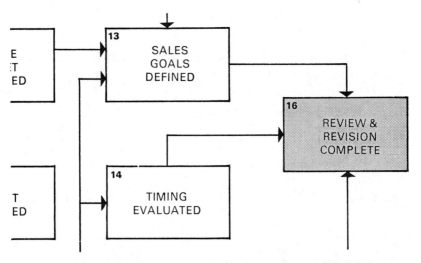

OBJECTIVE: Re-evaluate the Entire Concept Phase and Revise It Where Necessary.

Before one starts to prepare "The Plan," a thorough rethinking of each of "The Concept" milestones is in order. The entrepreneur must insure in his own mind that all the parts of "The Concept" jigsaw fit together.

THE PLAN

The objective of the plan is to formalize in detail the organization of the business with the minimum dollar outlay.

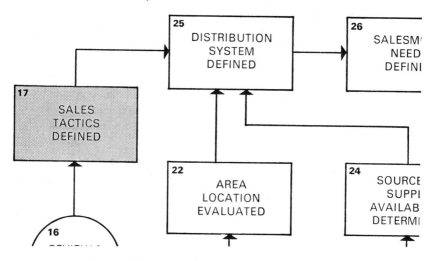

OBJECTIVE: Identify the Marketing Techniques to Be Utilized in
Attacking the Market.

From the sales-goals-defined milestone in "The Concept" phase,
sales was quantitatively defined. In this milestone we are concerned
with how the entrepreneur will attack the market. Sales tactics include the marketing effort from defining what types of salesmen
will be used to deciding what methods of advertising will be employed.

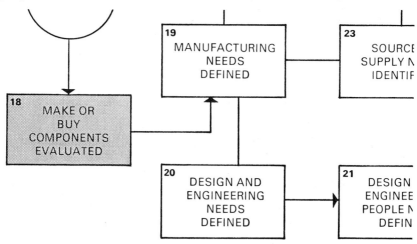

OBJECTIVE: Determine at the Very Outset Which, If Any, Components Will be Subcontracted to Other Organizations.

The main advantage with subcontracting is that, in general, the
entrepreneur will be able to have a fixed price per unit, or at least a

fixed price per component. If he intends to set up his own manufacturing facilities, he may find that his actual costs exceed his intended cost by 100-200%. Such *cost overruns are not infrequent with new ventures.* Accordingly, components or products should be subcontracted if at all possible.

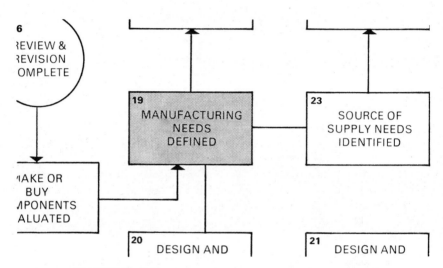

OBJECTIVE: Delineate Both Space and Machine Requirements in Order to Produce the Product.

With both the product clearly identified (see product identification milestone in "The Concept") as well as a decision made on which components or products to subcontract, the entrepreneur is now in a position to evaluate his manufacturing needs. Space requirements should not only take into account the next few months' production needs, but also those production needs as shown in the sales goals for the next three to five years. The same may be said for the machinery and other fixed asset needs. At this point it is appropriate to mention the "gearing up" syndrome. *Many businessmen, who have failed, have failed because they "geared up" for a production that never was needed.* The entrepreneur should buy only those machines and lease only that space which is required for the immediate future. However, he must make plans for what will happen a year to five years down the road when his production needs meet his sales goals.

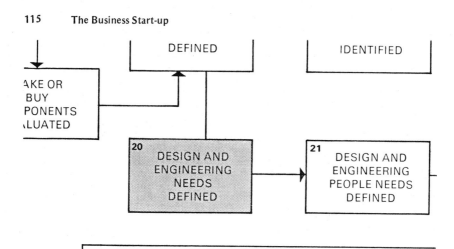

OBJECTIVE: Define Specific Engineering Skills and Hardware
Required to Produce the Product or Service.

This milestone does not include a definition of the people required from an engineering standpoint, but rather a definition of the
skills that the people must have in order to research, design, engineer,
and develop the product. Also included is an evaluation of the hardware required. If a great deal of research and development is required,
the entrepreneur may find that the hardware costs far exceed the
skill costs.

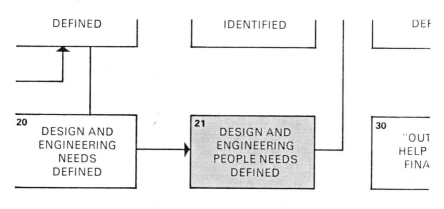

OBJECTIVE: Clearly Define How Many and What Types of People
Are Needed to Complete the Design and Engineering Requirements.

With the design and engineering needs clearly defined, the identification of types of people required becomes easy to define. If the product or the service is new or highly unusual, the design and engineering skills required may be unusually costly. This is especially true if the product will require a great deal of research and development. If, on the other hand, a similar product already exists or a product that requires the same type of process already exists, it may be possible to find engineering talent familiar with the requirements of the product.

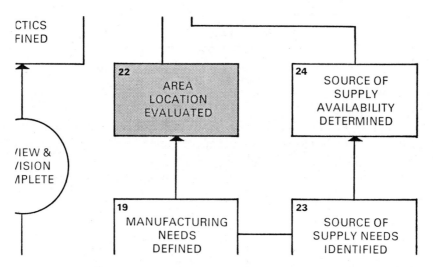

OBJECTIVE: Evaluate the Potential Headquarters and Plant Location Sites.

Economics, not esthetic or personal preferences, should rule as the prime factor in the choice of location. Of special significance will be the local labor rates as well as the local availability of talent. Cost of living should also be determined for a specific area, since wage and salary rates will be reflected with the geography. In general, the southeastern portion of the United States has relatively low wage and salary rates, while the northeastern section of the United States has possibly the highest cost of living. A publication of the Bureau of Labor Statistics, available at a local library, will give specifics regarding geographic cost differences in the United States.

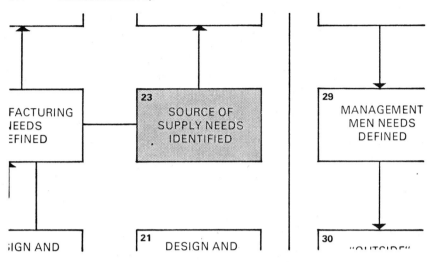

OBJECTIVE: Identify the Types of Raw Materials and Purchased
Inventory that Will Be Needed to Complete the Production.

With the product clearly identified, as well as a definition of
manufacturing needs, the entrepreneur should be in a good position
to make a list of materials needed for the manufacture of the product. Other needs such as office supplies and other overhead items
are, in most cases, intuitively apparent.

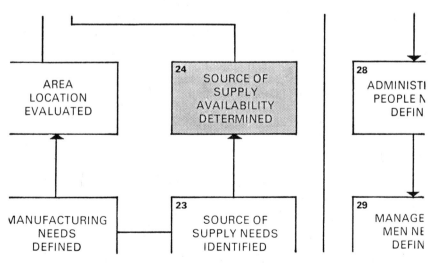

OBJECTIVE: Determine the Availability of Economic Sources of
Supply.

With the area of location evaluated plus the source of supply needs clearly defined, the direction is clear for determining what sources of supply are actually available. In a relatively small market this may be accomplished by turning to one's local Chamber of Commerce. On a broader scale, this could necessitate a nationwide search for those locations which would have the raw materials. At this juncture it may be apparent that a new area will have to be located. This may seem obvious from the economic factors surrounding the sources of supply. If such is the case, the entrepreneur must reevaluate his choice of area.

II. THE PL

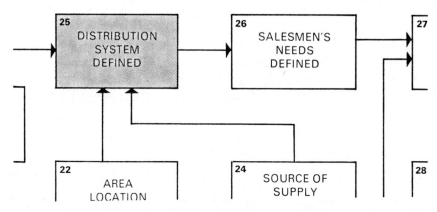

OBJECTIVE: Define How the Product or Service Will Be Transmitted from the Point of Manufacture or Creation to the Point of Sale.

Having previously defined the sales tactics, the specific area location, and the source of supply availability within the relevant geographic area, the distribution system is simple to construct. The distribution system should be as specific as possible, including how many and what types of middlemen will be utilized in order to obtain the sales required.

II. THE PLAN

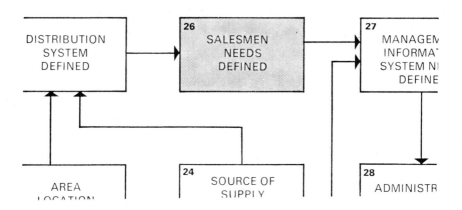

OBJECTIVE: Pinpoint Exactly What Types and How Many Salesmen Will Be Needed, When They Will Be Needed, and Where They Will Be Located.

Once the distribution system is clearly defined, along with the complete inventory of sales tactics taken, the numbers and types of salesmen become apparent. If the entrepreneur is going to go directly to the ultimate consumer, it may be necessary for him to set up a geographically dispersed sales network. If, on the other hand, he is going through middlemen or selling directly to a few industrial users, a traveling headquarters sales force may be all that is required. "If you can sell anything, you can sell everything" is still somewhat true today; however, many sales in a highly sophisticated market require not only the people interaction qualities that are necessary for all salesmen, but also an in-depth technical knowledge of the product or service. The more specialized and highly complex the product or service, the more difficult it will be to obtain highly qualified sales personnel.

II. THE PLAN

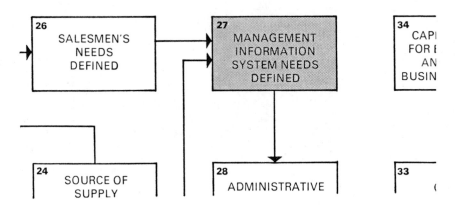

OBJECTIVE: Clearly Identify What Information Is Needed for Control Purposes as Well as Tax Purposes.

The tax laws in the United States are usually very specific in their requirements for a business. A competent certified public accountant will be able to define exactly what is needed, how often it is needed, and in what form the data is needed. This is a relatively simple task. Defining exactly what information is needed for control purposes is not so easy. *The entrepreneur should select a few cost items which are of extreme significance and which have the potential for varying greatly.* In most manufacturing concerns this will be a control of labor. If this is the case, a management information system must require that labor be controlled on a daily basis. In certain other industries other costs will be of more significance and have a greater potential for varying. In these cases, the management information system should target its efforts on those costs. Other costs that the management information system should produce may not be needed on a real-time basis, but a month or two lag may be sufficient. Perhaps only ballpark figures are needed.

The management information system should go beyond just mere costs. Changing market conditions, employee morale, and future technological possibilities should be among other variables included.

A periodic monitoring of these factors will help insure that the entrepreneur does not become caught off guard by a rapid shift of market conditions.

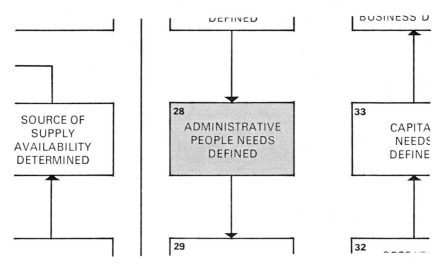

OBJECTIVE: Define How Many and What Type of Overhead People Are Needed.

With the number of production people needed defined, the number of engineering people needed defined, and the numbers and location of salesmen defined, the entrepreneur is now ready to evaluate the number and type of administrative people required to implement the management information system. Emphasis must be put on supporting the production people as opposed to management people. The reader will note that the management man's needs have not been discussed to this point. *Most new organizations start from the top and work down. This is inherently incorrect. The correct process is to work from the product and work up towards management.* Accordingly, the administrative staff is for the support of the production people who are, in turn, the support for the product.

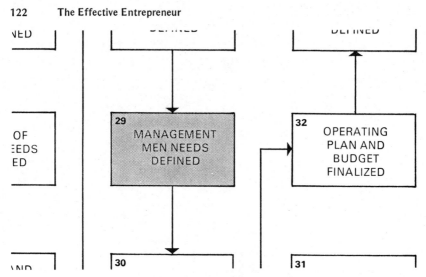

OBJECTIVE: Quantify How Many and What Types of Management Men Are Needed for the Business.

With the organization in place from the bottom up through the other overhead people, the number and types of management men needed are easily apparent. It may be, as in most cases with a new business, that only two or three really "key" management men are needed. An important point must be made at this juncture. The business must have a comptroller. Most entrepreneurs are not experts in finance. Many have a distinct distaste for the expertise required of a financial man. *The second most important man in a new enterprise, beyond the entrepreneur himself, is the financial vice president. As a general rule, no attempt at a new business of any substantial size should be started without a strong and experienced financial manager.*[1]

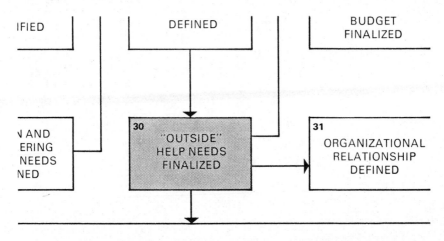

OBJECTIVE: Finalize Exactly What Type of Outside Help Is Needed.

With the complete internal organization finalized, an objective look must be taken at the organization to define those areas in which it will need help. Management consultants may be hired for almost any and every need a company might have. It is doubtful that the internal organization will have a full-time attorney or certified public accountant, and these men may have to be retained on an "as needed" basis. Another important point must be made at this juncture. That is, *outside management counseling is as important as in-house talent in determining entrepreneurial success or failure.*[2] A few years ago this was not the case. Today, with rapidly expanding knowledge and change, it becomes essential to the success of the entrepreneur that he enlist the aid of outside experts. The best source of these outside experts should be highly qualified and objective people on the board of directors.

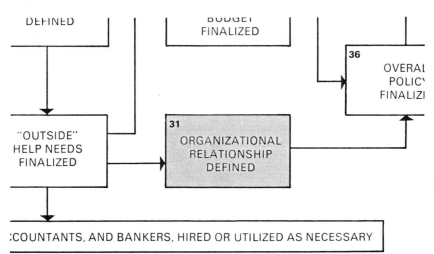

OBJECTIVE: Piece Together the People Relationships of the Business.

The organization has been built from the bottom up. All of the people needs have been defined, both internal and external, and the organization chart and relationships associated with that chart can now be made. In a new business several reporting relationships should be deemed appropriate, as opposed to the traditional "chain of command" type of approach. It may appear to the entrepreneur that since the business is so small, no organizational relationship need be defined. However, it is the authors' experience that *some sort of relationship must be defined*, even though one man may report to several different "bosses" and have the flexibility to "jump" his superior to get the job done.

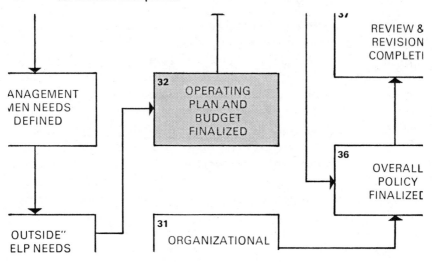

OBJECTIVE: Prepare in Detail a Cash Flow, Pro Forma Income
Statement, and Balance Sheets.

*Cash flow is much more important to predict and formalize than
either the income statement or the balance sheet.* Cash flow should
be on at least a monthly basis and should make all reasonable assumptions associated with the business. Many entrepreneurs make up
two sets of cash flows. One set being the worst possible condition
that could happen, and the second set being what he actually believes will happen. Items such as potential cost overruns, a detailed
analysis of direct cost and overhead, payout schedules, and billing
schedules must be taken into account. Pro forma income statements,

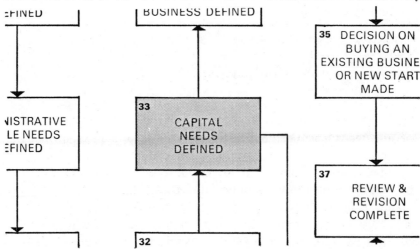

OBJECTIVE: Determine How Much Money Is Needed to Make the
Business Go.

balance sheets, and cash flow beyond 12 months should be made on a yearly basis for between three and five years into the future.

Once the operating plan and budget have been finalized, the capital needs become readily apparent from the cash flow. The entrepreneur must consider and utilize various sources of capital effectively. This includes pure debt, equity, living off his suppliers, advanced billings, and other forms of financing. The true entrepreneur will find various means to use different sources of capital in different ways.

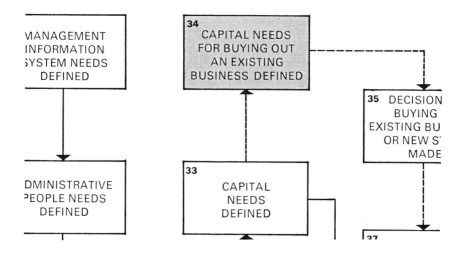

OBJECTIVE: Decide How Much and What Type of Capital Is Needed for Buying Out an Existing Business.

This milestone is enclosed with a dashed line to indicate that, in many cases, it will not be pursued. Oftentimes the entrepreneur overlooks the obvious solution to a new manufacturing or new service start-up: buying an already existing business. If one decides to buy a similar or related type of business, which will manufacture the product or supply the service that the entrepreneur plans to sell, the first consideration must be that of economics. The entrepreneur must find out through the process of negotiation exactly how much the present owner or the present stockholders of the business require and in what form the payment must be made. In some cases it may be feasible to buy an existing business for a net worth. In cases such as these it is not uncommon for the entrepreneur to pledge all the assets to a bank, obtain an 80-90% amount from the bank on the assets, and pay off the present stockholders with the money from the bank. This could result in the entrepreneur actually putting out no cash of his own in order to buy an existing business. The payout, of course, would be to the bank. Another alternative with stockholders may be a payout of future profits of the business. In any event, a decision regarding the capital needs for buying an existing business must be made.

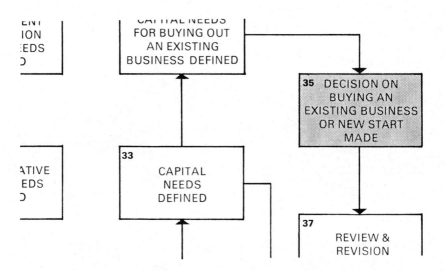

OBJECTIVE: Decide Whether a New Start or the Buying of an Existing Business Is More Economical for the Entrepreneur.

If it is at all possible, the entrepreneur should buy an existing business. This must be tempered, of course, with the understanding that the present business has a positive momentum and good people and facilities are present. *It is much easier to take an existing business and point it in a certain direction than to make a completely fresh start. However, most entrepreneurs are excited by the challenge and by the opportunity to make a fresh start. Thus, few entrepreneurs travel this route.*

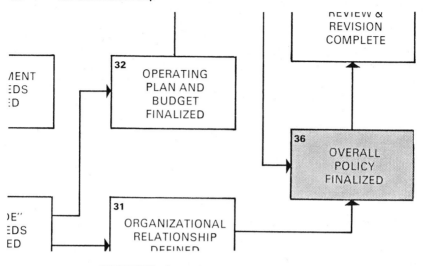

OBJECTIVE: Put on Paper Guidelines for Decisions.

A policy statement should be made on all strategic areas of the business. A policy is not a procedure. A procedure tells one how to do something. Procedures would be included in the management information system. The policies will spell out for others in a decision-making role those guidelines which the entrepreneur sets out in order to obtain the business objective.

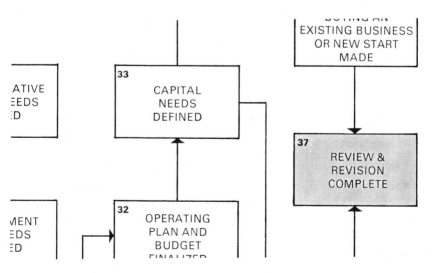

OBJECTIVE: Insure that the Plan Is Realistic.

Each milestone in "The Plan" must be completely thought out again in detail. The entrepreneur himself must intuitively feel that each of the milestone gears mesh into a cohesive plan. As many as five or six iterations of the complete plan process may be necessary before a comfortable feeling is obtained.

Each and every milestone of the plan must be completed and must be formalized on paper. An entrepreneur's eagerness may thrust him into the implementation; however, it is the authors' experience that many mistakes, much time, and money can be saved if in fact both "The Concept" and "The Plan" have been completely formalized and all reasonable revisions have taken place.

THE IMPLEMENTATION

The objective of "the implementation" is to carry out "The Plan" in an orderly, but rapid fashion.

Implementation is difficult. Very few things in business are ever implemented entirely according to plan. The milestones presented in the implementation should be followed as closely as possible; however, it is realized that in many instances some may have to be skipped for a time or the entire sequence may have to be rearranged.

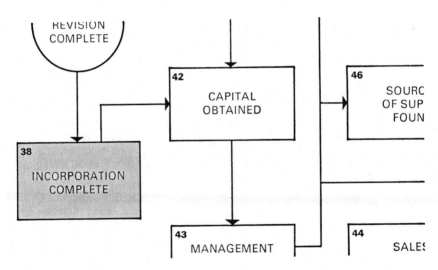

OBJECTIVE: Insure that the Business Is Incorporated.

An attorney should be consulted to insure that the incorporation is conducted in an expeditious manner. A certified public accountant should be consulted before the actual incorporation procedures are complete, since some states will have certain tax advantages over others. The tax structure is a function of whether one will or will not be engaged in interstate commerce, the potential business tax bracket, and, of course, the laws in each of the various states.

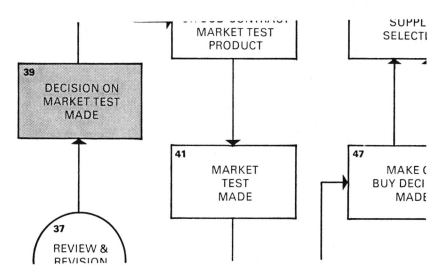

OBJECTIVE: Insure that a Conscious Decision Has Been Made on Whether or Not to Test the Market.

The entrepreneur must evaluate whether or not there is an economic advantage in going through the process of conducting a market test. Many entrepreneurs will consider their whole business venture a market test and completely omit this step. However, he should at least consider the alternative of putting his foot in the water before he jumps in.

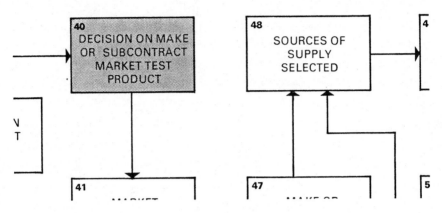

OBJECTIVE: Insure that a Conscious Decision Is Made on Whether to Manufacture or Subcontract the Product Used for the Market Test.

If it has been decided to make a market test, *it is in general in the best interest of the entrepreneur and of the business to subcontract the market test product.* Initial cost may seem high, but should the market test prove successful, the long-term cost will prove minimal. If the market test proves unsuccessful, the loss in terms of the market test plus the manufacture of the test products is small in comparison to the amount of money that would have been lost by choosing an "all-out" approach.

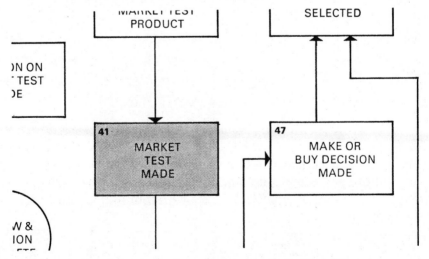

OBJECTIVE: Implement the Decision to Make a Market Test.

The market test must be of an extremely short duration, if for no other reason than that competitors might move in. The entrepreneur must be able to evaluate quickly whether his product or service is going to be readily accepted in the marketplace. The market test itself and the results should not take more than three months to complete. Even this short amount of time may appear to be too long to the entrepreneur, and he quite often will rush forward toward full implementation of the plan.

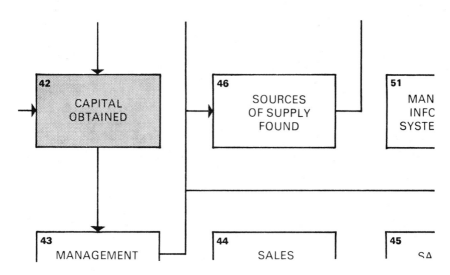

OBJECTIVE: Insure that the Capital Necessary to Run the Business Is Obtained.

The initial capital will, of course, be the entrepreneur's own equity. Additional capital may be in the form of stock which must be sold, debt, or perhaps some combination of both stock and debt. If one has to obtain debt, the best presentation that can be made to a bank would be to include both "The Concept" and "The Plan" sections of this business start-up model in complete detail. Various banks should be approached since the banking business is highly negotiable and views toward new business ventures differ markedly with the personalities involved.

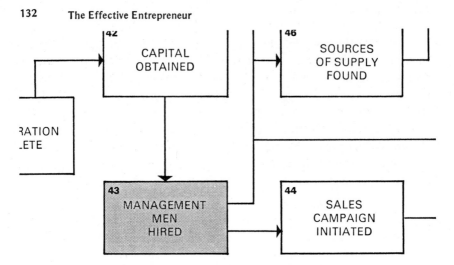

OBJECTIVE: Insure that the Organization Is Staffed from the Top Down.

The reader will recall that during "The Plan" the organization was built theoretically from the bottom up. With the organizational relationship defined in "The Plan," *the entrepreneur is now in a position to staff his organization from the top down.* The first step, therefore, is the hiring and training of his management people. As mentioned previously in one of the discussions in "The Plan," most new businesses have a few key management personnel. As also previously mentioned, a comptroller is essential.

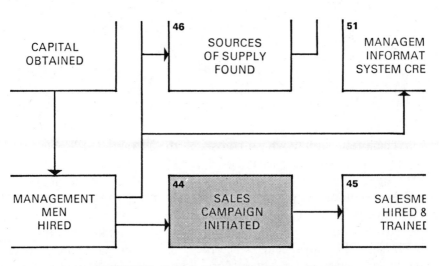

OBJECTIVE: Bring in Orders Just as Soon as Possible.

The first law of entrepreneurial survival is bringing profitable business in the door. It is not setting up the business, not setting up internal systems, not hiring the people to do the work, but rather it is bringing in business just as soon as possible. To the academic observer it may seem improper that the sales campaign be initiated long before salesmen are hired, the salesmen are trained, the production people are hired and trained, or the manufacturing facilities are set up. The authors agree that it would be a more orderly process to wait for the sales campaign; however, it must be recalled that *to get a business profitable, revenues must exceed expenses. There is only one way to produce revenues: sales.*

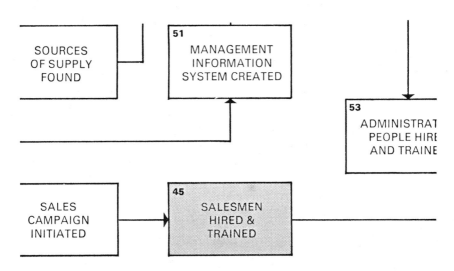

OBJECTIVE: Hire and Train the Sales Force.

The entrepreneur's initial sales force may be himself and a few other key employees. In all likelihood, the entrepreneur will himself be a natural salesman. For any additional people brought into the organization, he must insure that they have both the product knowledge as well as the interpersonal people skills required to do the job. Unless he is bringing a sales force with him, it may be best to go through some personnel consultants who are experienced in the hiring of superior salesmen.

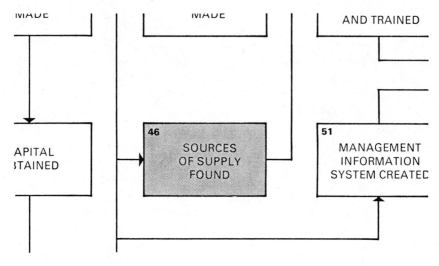

OBJECTIVE: Insure that the Various Sources of Supply Available
Are Located.

All possible sources of supply should be listed. A review as to
their stability, both financial and delivery, as well as their prices, must
be made.

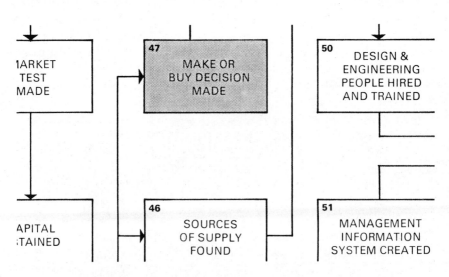

OBJECTIVE: Make the Final Decision as to Whether to Make or
Buy Components or Products.

The final decision must be made in terms of economics. If it appears that it is much more economical for the entrepreneur to make the product, then by all means he must do it. If, on the other hand, it appears that the costs are reasonably close to each other, then the decision to buy the components is in order. This is especially true in a market where there is a strong likelihood for a complete shift in consumer wants and needs.

III. THE IMPLEMENTATION

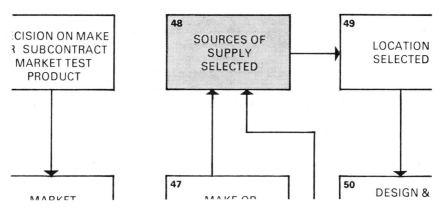

OBJECTIVE: Filter Down to Those Sources of Supply Which Will Do Business with the Entrepreneur.

A basic decision must be made as to whether the entrepreneur will use one or more sources of supply for this same basic component or product. There are advantages and disadvantages to both. If one source of supply is utilized, there may be substantial price savings. However, if many sources of supply are utilized, there is the possibility if one goes on strike that the entrepreneur can obtain all of his supplies from these other sources.

III. THE IMPLEMENTATION

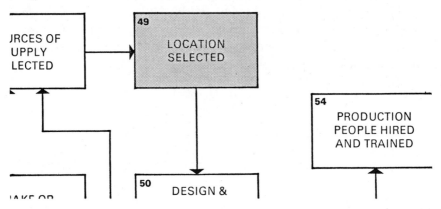

OBJECTIVE: Insure That a Fixed Location Is Selected.

The specific location must be made in terms of economics. The true entrepreneur will not go for the "best for the price" but rather for the least price. It must be recalled that the business is fighting for survival. This is a crucial period in the life of any business, and any expenditures over and above the absolute minimum must be curtailed.

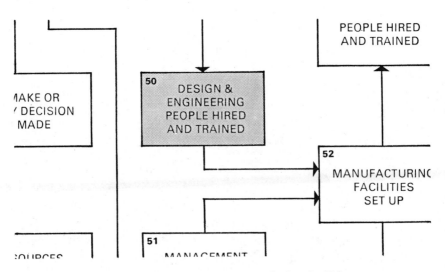

OBJECTIVE: Hire and Train Necessary Engineering Talent.

If an industry similar to the entrepreneur's business exists, then this should be the first source of obtaining any engineering people. If the product requires a great deal of research and development talent, there may be some difficulty in obtaining the men. Research and development talent is difficult to both hire and control since the research and development type of person usually prefers the security and orderliness of the large corporation as opposed to the frenzy and highly disorganized manner of an entrepreneur.

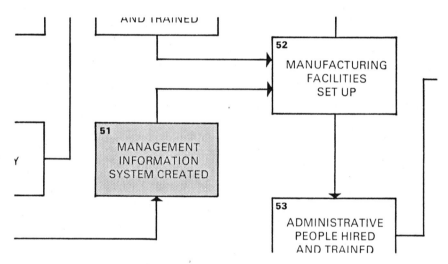

OBJECTIVE: Create and Implement the Administrative Paperwork System of the Business.

The management men must be the ones who create and imple-ment the management information system. The management infor-mation system is for their use and their benefit, and it is important that the system not be "pre-created" before the management team is in place. It may seem to some that the management information sys-tem should have been created back in "The Plan;" however, the new business start-up essentially revolves around the entrepreneur and a few key people, and it is vital that these people have the responsibil-ity for creating the system which will help them control the business.

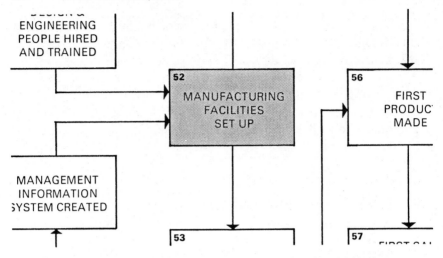

OBJECTIVE: Implement the Manufacturing and Engineering Needs in Terms of Space and Machinery.

The production facility should be set up as quickly as possible with the management men responsible for the plant layout. If the plant is to be of a large size, it may be necessary for outside management consulting talent to be used. In most cases it is sufficient for the management personnel to sit down and logically lay out the flow of work. *It is more important in this period of a business life to get something that works right away than to be concerned whether or not it works at a 100% efficiency.*

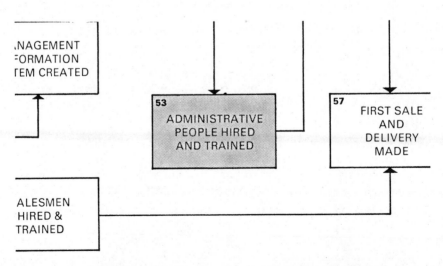

OBJECTIVE: Hire and Train the Overhead Administrative People.

In most cases a newspaper ad will bring in enough talented clerical and secretarial type people. In very few markets in the United
States is there a severe shortage of either clerical or secretarial talent.
An excellent source for this type of personnel is the U.S. Armed
Forces. Men in the Armed Forces, especially those who have been in
for quite a period of time, may be experienced at the detail requirements for such a position.

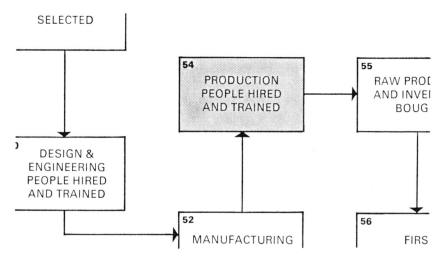

OBJECTIVE: Hire and Train the Production People.

In conjunction with the hiring and training of the administrative
people, management must take upon itself the responsibility for hiring and training of the production people. The same statement may
be made about production people as was made about design and engineering people; that is, if there is an industry which is similar to
that of the entrepreneur's, it may be possible to induce production
people away from competitors. The difficulty one will have in hiring
production people is that the entrepreneur's new business is unstable
and may involve a high degree of risk. It is not uncommon during this
stage of the business life for the entrepreneur to find that he must
hire and turn over as many as 40 people in order to get three good
ones.

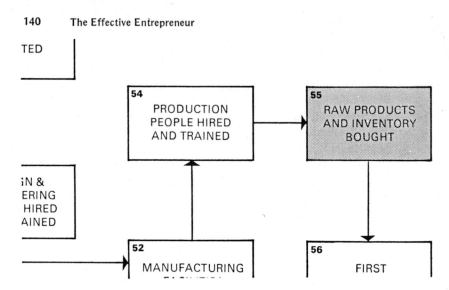

OBJECTIVE: Buy All the Raw Products Necessary for the First Production Run.

With the sources of supply clearly identified in the previous steps, the buying of the raw products is a matter of pure implementation. Reasonable but not excessive inventory positions should be initiated.

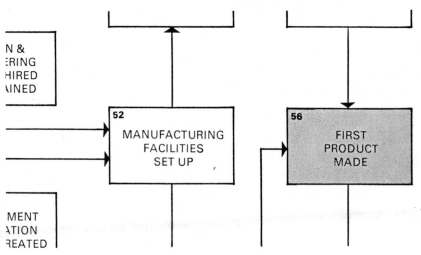

OBJECTIVE: Make the First Product.

The first production run should be viewed by the entire management team, as well as any consultants which the entrepreneur has retained concerning production. The first production run is exceedingly important and oftentimes difficult for all concerned. It is imperative, therefore, that extreme care and *attention to detail be taken.*

MENT
\TION
REATED

```
                         53                      57
                         ADMINISTRATIVE          FIRST SALE
                         PEOPLE HIRED            AND
                         AND TRAINED             DELIVERY
                                                 MADE
```

/IEN
' &
ED

OBJECTIVE: Sale and Delivery of the First Product.

The first sale should be a momentous mark for all concerned in the entrepreneur's business. Care should be taken to insure that the delivery is made to the customer's satisfaction and the product meets all the specifications and desire that the customer has expressed.

This completes the business start-up model. This model, if used as a base for all new entrepreneurs starting new businesses, will provide a meaningful road map to get the business off to the fastest possible start. As was mentioned in the introduction of this book, the entrepreneur's greatest strength lies in his ability to get a business started off quickly. His effectiveness is usually diminished thereafter. The Concept, The Plan, and The Implementation phases, if properly interpreted and followed, will increase the effectiveness of the entrepreneur in his business venture. Perhaps Toffler best described the entrepreneurial heritage:

> The free-swinging entrepreneur who started up vast enterprises unafraid of defeat or adverse opinion, is a folk hero of industrialism, particularly in the United States. Pareto labeled the entrepreneurs adventurous souls, hungry for novelty . . . not at all alarmed at change.[3]

NOTES

[1] University of Toronto, School of Business Tapes "Seminar on Venture Capital," Time, Inc., 1972.

[2] Ibid.

[3] Alvin Toffler, *Future Shock,* Random House, 1970, p. 148.

8

**THE
ENTREPRENEUR
IN
PERSPECTIVE**

In the concluding chapter of this book, the authors take the opportunity to place the entrepreneur in his crucial role in the American economic system. This requires that this book be viewed in perspective. That is, its niche be defined in light of the dynamic nature of American entrepreneurial activity.

Sixty British executives who visited the United States in search of ways to rebuild their war-torn economy reported: "If there is one secret above all of the American achievements in productivity, it is to be found in the attitude of American management."[1] The visitors attribute this attitude to four factors:

1. The spirit of the frontier has fostered the sense of opportunity that pervades American industrial and community life.

2. Faith in business and the individual reflects the high esteem with which the businessman is regarded in the American community.

3. The ideal of competition leads "even those companies which are not operating in a highly competitive market tend to run their enterprises as though they were."

4. Belief in change prevents a successful experiment from crystallizing into accepted custom, whereas an unsuccessful experiment is accepted as an occupational risk and is set against the experience to be gained.

This self-confident, aggressive attitude can only operate in a highly competitive environment. In fact, this attitude tends to make the American economic system even more competitive. The interaction between American Capitalism, government, consumers, and business explains much of the economic success we all enjoy.

Economic theorists, trying to determine those factors necessary for the dynamic operation of a competitive market economy, point to the crucial role of the entrepreneur. A competitive environment is maintained, they theorize, by entry or threat of entry of new firms. If, for example, a group of firms that comprise an industry becomes less than highly competitive, new firms enter the industry to garner some of the excess profits. As more and more new firms enter, the excess profits dwindle and the older firms become more competitive or fade from the scene. As every entrepreneur and economist recognizes, however, this view of competition is oversimplified. One major point not covered is the idea that certain barriers exist to easy entry

of new firms. The most often cited barriers are financial and technological. For example, the financial and technological problems associated with establishing a new automobile manufacturing firm to
compete with G.M., Ford, and Chrysler are mind-boggling.

Barriers to entry in other industries, of course, are much lower.
Restaurants, repair shops, and gift shops are but a few which fall into
this category. Businessmen, economists, government bureaucrats, and
politicians, recognizing the importance of entrepreneurial activity,
have become quite concerned with these barriers — not only their
height, but also how they have changed over time. For example, when
the automobile industry was in its infancy the barriers to entry were
not great, as evidenced by the number of firms which comprised the
industry. Such names as the Stutz Bearcat, Pierce Arrow and the
Tucker are the last reminders of that bygone era. The automobile
industry illustrates the general, but not universal, trend of a gradual
increase in these barriers over time.

Concern for the height of these barriers should be found in all
quarters of our society interested in preserving the competitive
nature of our capitalistic economic system. For it is the entrepreneur
who stands at one of the cornerstones.

The authors take this opportunity to describe briefly the nature
of these barriers existing in our contemporary society and how they
are changing over time. The remainder of this chapter is devoted to
this purpose.

ENTREPRENEURIAL TALENT BARRIERS

The first barrier to entry actually needs little discussion because it is
the subject of this book. The central theme has been that due to a
number of unique forces in the entrepreneurial environment, not all
people are destined to be successful entrepreneurs.

Chapter 2 described the nature of the entrepreneurial environment and Chapter 3 the nature of the forces motivating entrepreneurs. Consistent with the writings of McClelland and Hagen, the
authors conclude that entrepreneurs are people with an extremely
high need to achieve. In Chapters 4 and 5, entrepreneurial management styles and behavioral characteristics were described. The
authors conclude that entrepreneurs have a fairly unique set of styles
and characteristics. Some of these can be learned, but many, such as
ego drive and empathy balance, cannot.

For these reasons, the authors contend that one barrier to entrepreneurial activity is the existence of people with these necessary sets of characteristics. Fortunately for the American economy, the existence of an adequate number of entrepreneurs has not been a serious problem. The major problem has been identifying successful entrepreneurs. For the individual considering entrepreneurial pursuits, to be able to evaluate his personal strengths and weaknesses and make a rational decision is one aspect of the problem. Another is for investors in entrepreneurs to be able to evaluate and predict the probability of success. The ultimate justification for the expenditure of time and effort in writing *The Effective Entrepreneur* is to help alleviate this problem.

Chapters 6 and 7 were designed to aid the student to understand the nature of the problems faced by the entrepreneur and how he might go about solving them. For the potential entrepreneur they serve as guidelines or road maps to assist him in making that new business successful.

FINANCIAL BARRIERS

Any discussion of barriers to entrepreneurial activity must include financial barriers. The authors have observed that there is always capital available for the outstanding entrepreneur. Perhaps the capital is not available on the terms the entrepreneur wants, but the dollar value is there. It must be remembered that the way the entrepreneur succeeds is that he decides what he wants to do and then he figures out how to do it. Raising capital is only a small step in the business start-up and is only part of the implementation of what the entrepreneur wants to do.

In passing it should be noted that there are several forces operating in our economic system which tend to make capital more available to the entrepreneur. For example, the controversial capital gains tax tends to encourage private investors to consider higher risk investments which have promise of rapid internal growth. Similarly, the highly competitive nature of American industry places a premium on the discovery of innovative new methods and products which are frequently associated with entrepreneurial activity. Ten years ago only 40 of *Fortune's* 500 largest corporations had a policy of investing in new ventures. Today that figure has risen to 175.

TECHNOLOGICAL BARRIERS

The existence and direction of technological barriers to entrepreneurial activity are less well defined than in most other areas. In the larger and more stable industries such as steel and automobiles, it appears that the barriers are large and increasing. Firms in these industries employ large research and development staffs whose function is to keep the firm in an advanced technological position. In the case of rapidly growing industries such as electronics, the frequent entrance of new firms indicates the barriers are not as high.

The smaller service industries, on the other hand, have traditionally been, and still are, the primary domain of entrepreneurial activity. This was discussed extensively in Chapter 6.

GOVERNMENTAL BARRIERS

For obvious reasons the official policy of the Federal Government is to encourage small business and entrepreneurial activity. The Small Business Investment Company Act (SBIC) of 1958 is only one example.

Unfortunately for small businessmen, the Federal and local Governments have developed other policies which are creating barriers to entry for the entrepreneur. The most serious of these relate to the myriad of laws and regulations concerning how a business must report its activities.

For example, the following list includes some of the more important government-related laws and regulations with which the entrepreneur must comply.

A. City

Business License

Zoning Restrictions

B. State

Sales Tax Reporting

Unemployment Bureau Reporting

Workers Compensation Insurance

Environmental Impact Studies

Income Taxes

C. Federal

Payroll Tax Reporting

Social Security Reporting

Quarterly Income Taxes

Unemployment Taxes

While this list is not complete, the important point is that the entrepreneur must comply with all these governmental regulations. Failure to do so usually results in devastating penalties or large lump-sum payments due at a later date. The number of new firms that have failed due to these kinds of problems is unknown, but in the opinion of the authors it is sizeable.

If a new firm should need venture capital from an SBIC, the problems are increased by the legal complications imposed by the Federal Government. A team of specialized lawyers is usually required to steer a path through the pitfalls which are present.

To deal effectively with all the government barriers, entrepreneurs are faced more and more with the requirement of retaining legal advice and professional accounting service. For this reason alone, the rise of franchising as a way of decreasing the risk of starting a new business is easily explained.

It has been suggested that new business be given a moratorium on many government regulations in order to increase the success rate. Dr. Paul Harmon commented on one aspect of this possibility in his study of SBIC's ". . . the tax problem should be mentioned since the purpose of the legislation (SBIC act of 1958) was to induce venture capital into small new firms with growth potential. If tax rates are discouraging the flow of such capital, then legislation must be devised which will counteract this one way or another."[2]

While these and other barriers to entry are changing over time, other forces are at work which tend to mitigate their effect. Probably the most significant force has been the rise of the franchising concept.

The importance of this force can be seen in the estimate that by 1979 at least 60% of all businesses will be some sort of franchise. The franchisor can employ the necessary resources to overcome the governmental, technological, and to a degree, financial barriers. Franchisors are also one of the groups most interested in the evaluation of potential entrepreneurs in order to select those who possess the psychological characteristics to succeed. It is hoped that this book will make a contribution in this area.

Another force which has developed in recent years is societal concern for minority entrepreneurs. The reasoning has been that the only way to include minorities in the mainstream of American life is for minorities to share in the economic system. This requires that they assume entrepreneurial activity.

To date this concern and the resulting social forces have not met with outstanding success. It has been shown that the environment in some foreign countries is not conducive to the high ego drive/empathy required to be a successful entrepreneur. Perhaps the same can be said for the American society with regard to minorities. That is, up until the 60's the environment in the American scene was not conducive to many people in the minority population gaining the high ego drive and high empathy necessary. If many of the minority enterprises do fail over the next few years, the innate psychological make-up may well be the reason. Despite massive government assistance programs, such as the Minority Enterprise Small Business Investment Companies (MESBIC), it may well take a full generation starting with the children born in the early 60's before a proper minority entrepreneurial psychological makeup can be achieved.

NOTES

[1]*Advanced Management*, October 1955, page 30.

[2]Dr. Paul Lewis Harmon, *An Analysis of the Investment Policies of the Small Business Investment Companies*, January 1963, unpublished PhD dissertation, UCLA, page 56.

APPENDIX

In Dible's thoroughly enjoyable and informative book *Up Your Own Organization*[1] there appear several checklists used by some of the most outstanding professional management consulting and venture capital firms in the United States. The reader will find these checklists an additional aid to Chapter 7.

BUSINESS START-UP CHECKLIST

Dible has used material from the New York Management Center, Inc. in compiling this checklist.

A. Place of Small Business

1. What are the most serious problems for the small businessman?

2. How would these affect *you* as a business owner?

B. Employment or Your Own Business

1. Would you worry less as someone else's employee or as owner of your own business?

2. What is your principal reason for wanting to enter business on your own?

C. Factors in Business Success

1. Have you rated yourself and had some acquaintances rate you on the qualities necessary for success as your own boss?

2. Have you taken steps to improve yourself in those qualities in which you are weak but which are needed for success?

3. Have you saved money, made business contacts, taken special courses, or read particular books for the purpose of preparing yourself for business ownership?

4. Have you had experience in your proposed line of business or in one similar to it?

5. Have you employed and supervised workers?

6. Are you (a) good at managing your own time and energy?

(b) easily discouraged? (c) willing to work harder in your own business than as someone else's employee?

D. Appraising a Going Concern

1. Have you checked the proposition against the lists of warnings issued by Better Business Bureaus?

2. Have you honestly compared the expense of starting a similar business of your own with the price asked for the business you are considering buying?

3. Has your lawyer checked to see that the title is good and that there are no liens against the business and no past due taxes or public utility bills?

4. If it is a bulk sale, has the Bulk Sales Law been complied with?

5. Have you earnestly investigated possible developments that might affect the business adversely?

E. Justifying the New Business

1. If your new firm will be similar to established businesses, have you checked all available data?

2. If your business will be based on an entirely new idea, have you attempted to secure actual contracts or commitments from potential customers instead of merely getting their polite approval of your idea?

3. Have you discussed your proposition with competent advisors who are in several different occupations or who have different, but important, viewpoints?

F. Financing and Organizing the Business

1. Have you written down a complete, itemized list of all capital needs for starting your kind of business, including a fair allowance for operating expenses, your own living ex-

penses until the business is able to support itself, *and* a substantial reserve for the one serious error most businessmen make during their first year of operation?

2. Have you discussed this financial prospectus with a banker and a successful businessman in your proposed field?

3. If available for your kind of business, have you used as guides the U.S. Department of Commerce publications?

4. Are you sure you have made ample provisions for your personal and family needs during the period when no funds should be withdrawn from the business?

5. Have you considered all the factors for and against each legal form of organization?

6. If you plan to secure much of your initial capital from friends or relatives, are you *certain* that your business will remain free of "friendly" domination?

G. Selecting the Profitable Location

1. Have you compared several different possible locations before making your final choice?

2. Have you used one or more detailed checklists to guide your selection?

3. Have you arranged for legal counsel before signing the lease and any similar contracts?

4. Are you and the affected members of your family satisfied that the community in which you plan to locate will be a desirable place to live and to rear your children?

5. If your proposed location is not almost ideal, are there sound reasons (not merely your impatience to get started) why you should not wait and try to secure a more nearly ideal location?

H. Building and Layout

1. Have you studied your proposed building with function, construction, and modernization in mind?

2. Have you made a personal inspection of the physical plant of other successful businesses similar to the one you plan to start, including both independents and branches of large organizations?

3. Have you planned your proposed layout for the building to scale on paper?

4. If the proposed building does not meet all of your important needs, are there any *good* reasons for deciding to use it?

I. Establishing the Business Policies

1. Have you made an honest, objective investigation of the probable success of your proposed policies?

2. Have you written down the main provisions of your general and major policies?

3. Have you discussed your proposed policies with competent advisors to counteract the beginner's tendency to offer what *he* likes and wants instead of what his potential *customers* like and want?

4. Have you written down an adequate statement of the reputation you want your business to acquire with customers, suppliers, and competitors?

5. Have you made adequate provisions to insure that your policies will be understood and enforced and that you will receive ample warning of the need for policy adjustments?

J. Management and Leadership

1. Have you planned the way you will organize duties and responsibilities?

2. Have you made up a tentative plan or schedule to guide the distribution of your own time and effort?

3. Have you planned ways to conserve your time and energy by using management aids such as policies, standards, budgets, and schedules?

4. Have you provided some check on your own actions to insure that you do adequate management planning before making commitments or important decisions covering future activities of the business?

5. Have you arranged to use periodically some checklist covering detailed activities regarding customer relations, maintenance, safety, or whatever type of activity that will require close attention to details in your particular business?

K. Employee Relations

1. Have you investigated thoroughly the advisability of employing friends and relatives as compared to employing persons only on the basis of objectively determined qualifications?

2. Have you planned working conditions to be as desirable and practical as possible? Are you sure that what *you* think will be pleasant will also be pleasant to your employees?

3. Are you certain the employee incentives you plan to use represent what the workers want rather than what *you* think they want?

4. Have you planned your employment, induction, and follow-up procedures?

L. Relationships with Resources

1. Have you considered each of the desirable objectives in choosing a particular supplier before selecting the companies with which you plan to deal?

2. Have you carefully analyzed the points for and against concentrating your purchases with one or a few vendors, taking into account your personal skill and ability as well as conditions in your line of business?

3. Have you given adequate attention to each of the fundamentals of buying in making your plans for this function?

4. Have you investigated your field of business with reference to the presence and advantages of voluntaries or cooperative buying groups?

M. Sales Promotion

1. Have you analyzed your probable competition in connection with the direct and indirect sales promotional methods you plan to use?

2. Have you planned definite ways to build and maintain superior customer relations?

3. Have you defined your potential customers so precisely that you could describe them in writing?

4. Have you decided how you can measure and record the degree of success achieved with each sales promotion so that you can repeat the "hits" and avoid the "duds?"

5. Have you made provisions to secure a sales promotional calendar applicable to your kind of business?

6. Have you considered different features of your business that would be appropriate for special promotions timed to your customers' needs and interests?

N. Advertising for Profit

1. Have you put in writing your own list of "do's" and "don't's" to guide your advertising?

2. Have you made a list of all the media suitable for use in *your* business, with some evaluation of each?

3. Have you selected the most promising reasons why people should patronize your business and incorporated them in plans for your opening advertising?

4. Have you made use of all appropriate sources in the preparation of a good initial mailing list?

5. Have you given careful thought to the advertising value of the proposed names for your firm, products, and services?

6. Have you made plans for some unusual gesture of welcome and appreciation for all customers during the opening days of your business?

7. Have you planned how you can measure the effectiveness of your advertising?

8. Have you arranged to use an advertising checklist?

O. Pricing for Turnover and Profit

1. Have you thought through the desirability of and difficulties connected with acquiring the price/product image you plan for your business?

2. Have you considered the probable reaction of competitors to your pricing practices?

3. Have you compared the relative importance in your business of each major marketing instrument, including price?

4. Have you investigated possible legal limitations on your pricing plans?

5. Have you considered possible applications of price lining and brand lining to your business?

6. Have you decided on the formula or method you will use in pricing each class of goods and services?

7. Have you decided how and to what extent you will meet probable price competition?

P. Expense Control

1. Have you investigated the standard systems of expense classifications used in your field and selected the most appropriate one for your use?

2. Have you determined what are usually the largest items of expense for your type of business and made definite plans for controlling these expenses from the very beginning of the business?

3. Have you determined which, if any, expense items, though normally small for your type of business, very easily become excessively large unless carefully controlled *at all times?*

4. Have you prepared on paper a *flexible* expense budget for two or three different probable amounts of volume of business, including provisions for frequent operating expense reports to be compared with planned figures in your budget?

5. Have you determined the standard operating ratios for your field that you plan to use as guides?

6. Have you compared the expense of "farming out," or having certain activities of the business done by outside agencies, with what it would cost you to do the work yourself?

Q. Inventory or Stores Control

1. Have you determined carefully what constitutes a *balanced* inventory for your business?

2. Have you recorded on paper the exact information you will need for effective inventory control?

3. Have you planned the best methods for securing this information?

4. Have you selected the most appropriate inventory control *system* to use?

5. Have you planned the best procedures to use for stock- or stores-keeping?

6. Have you listed the purposes and uses of information you plan to secure from your inventory- or stores-control system?

R. Regulations and Taxes

1. Have you ascertained from reliable sources all regulations that must be complied with for your business?

2. Have you provided for an adequate system of record keeping that will furnish essential information for all taxation purposes?

3. Have you checked the police, health, fire, and other safety regulations that apply to your business?

4. Have you provided for securing all information from employees required by law?

5. Have you obtained a social security number?

6. Have you checked with competent advisors systems you plan to use in paying sales, excise, and similar taxes?

7. Have you complied with regulations governing the use of a firm or trade name, brand names, or trademarks?

S. Credit and Collections

1. Have you carefully investigated the need for credit extension by your business?

2. Have you planned specifically the various ways you will secure and use information obtainable from your charge-account customers?

3. Have you made a personal investigation of the services and costs of affiliating with the local credit bureau?

4. Have you planned the basic procedures you will *always* follow before extending credit to any applicant?

5. Have you formulated plans to *control* all credit accounts?

T. Records

1. Have you decided what records will be adequate for each division and need of your business?

2. Have you secured the necessary forms to enable you to start keeping adequate records from the first day of business operation?

3. Have you planned your record system so that appropriate use will be made of standard operating ratios?

4. Have you investigated the possibilities of using simplified record-keeping systems for some of your needs?

5. Have you considered applications of the "one-book" system to your business?

6. Have you decided when and by whom each record needed will be kept?

7. Have you investigated the advantages and cost of using some outside agency?

8. Have you made plans for keeping essential records in addition to your accounting records?

9. Have you investigated the record-keeping system recommended by the trade association in your field?

VENTURE CAPITAL CHECKLIST 1

Robert R. Kley Associates, Inc., has put together a checklist utilized in financing a new product venture.

1. Provide a one-page summary of the idea, the market need, and the amount of money required.

2. Describe the key goals and objectives — specify what you are setting out to achieve, particularly in the sense of sales and profitability.

3. Provide an in-depth market analysis, and cite external sources of market research data.

4. List the names of six close competitors.

5. List for each product the anticipated selling price to an ultimate consumer, and present a brief summary that compares these prices with those of major competitors.

6. Provide a list of potential customers who have expressed an interest in the proposed products.

7. Provide a one-page summary of the functional specifications for the new product.

8. Illustrate the physical forms of the products with drawings and/or photographs.

9. Provide a profile of the most important patents.

10. Categorize and list the key technologies and skills required to develop and manufacture the proposed products, and indicate which technologies and skills the company plans to emphasize.

11. Describe the alternative channels of sales distribution, e.g., direct sales, sales through manufacturers' representatives, sales through original equipment manufacturers (OEMs), etc.

12. Describe the basis for determining, from the purchaser's point of view, if the new products are typically "lease" or "buy" items.

13. Describe the type and geographical distribution of the anticipated field-service organization.

14. Describe the building-block modularity of the new products (a module is something which can be independently manufactured, is testable, and can be inventoried).

15. Portray the cost vs. volume curves for each module, and illustrate the cost breakdown for material, labor, and factory burden.

16. Describe the manufacturing process involved; illustrate it by means of a block diagram.

17. Describe the types and quantities of capital equipment needed, and determine when this equipment will be required.

18. Portray a Flow-Event-Logic-Feedback chart that illustrates achievement milestones and portrays stepped levels of when and how additional funds should go into the venture.

19. Project staff and plant space requirements over a five-year period.

20. List the rationale for choosing a particular manufacturing plant location.

21. Provide cash flow projections by month for 24 months and then every quarter for the following three years.

22. Provide pro-forma balance sheets for five years.

23. Provide pro-forma profit and loss statements for five years.

24. State the degree of ownership control being sought and the limits to which these can be varied in regard to time and profitability.

Several examples of growth industries to which this checklist has been applied are:

Health Sciences	Power and Energy
Education	Metals and Alloys

Computers and Peripherals   Chemicals and Plastics
Solid State Electronics   Pollution Control
Electronic Communications   Infrared, Optics, and Holography.

VENTURE CAPITAL CHECKLIST 2

If an entrepreneur wishes to receive financing from the Small Business Investment Company of New York, the first step would be to provide the following information.

1. Short introductory statement giving facts as to incorporation of company (date, state), location of executive offices, and *brief* description of business (what is made, how it is used, who uses it).

2. Statement regarding amount of funds needed from SBIC-NY and use to which said funds are to be put.

3. Statement regarding amount of capital already supplied by applicant. How much in cash? How much in the form of patents, processes, or property? How much as compensation for past services rendered?

4. Statement regarding capitalization of company, listing short-term debt, long-term debt, preferred stock, common stock, and surplus (or deficit). Specify interest rates and term on debt (options?).

5. Summary of earnings and a projection of earnings for coming years; also a cash flow statement if it seems appropriate.

6. More detailed outline of business, indicating products, method of manufacture, markets, method of sales, research and development, patents, competition, plant, property, equipment, and backlog.

7. Description of management, including previous experience, education, and age.

8. Accounting of remuneration of management if over $20,000 per year.

9. List of principal shareholders, with amounts held.

10. Audited financial statements for past five years or whatever is available.

VENTURE CAPITAL CHECKLIST 3

If an entrepreneur wishes to receive venture capital from Goodman and Mautner, a Los Angeles venture capital firm, he would have to provide the following information.

A. Corporate Structure

1. Give the name of the company, the state in which it was incorporated, and the date of its incorporation.

2. Predecessor companies: if any, give their particulars and their history up to the incorporation of the subject company.

3. Subsidiaries of subject: show the degree of ownership by the subject company and identify any minority interests. Also give the dates and state of the incorporation of any subsidiaries.

4. Outstanding securities, including bank loans involving the subject company and any subsidiaries that are not 100 percent in the ownership of the subject company: state the principal terms of such securities. Wherever bank loans or institutional obligations exist, identify lender, and name, if possible, the individual at the lending institution who is most familiar with the account.

5. Name and state the other holdings of the principal holders of subject company's common stock and/or other types of equity securities (convertible debt or preferred stock). If any such principal holders are not members of executive management, identify them and describe briefly the history and reasons for their stock purchases; also state if such holders have been in the past or are currently suppliers, vendees, or lessees, or if they have any other business relationships with the subject company. If they do have such relationships, describe them in full, including the financial details of any transactions with the subject company.

6. Give a chronological record of the subject company's sales of its equity securities, stating prices, number of buyers, identity of principal buyers, and any other pertinent facts.

B. Executive Management and Work Force

1. Provide an abbreviated schematic diagram of the organization.

2. Provide personal resumes, including academic and business backgrounds, of all executive officers and any other supervisory personnel who may be considered of special value to the organization (for example, director of research, production manager, etc.). Business backgrounds should be as specific as possible regarding the positions held and the functions of such positions. Name three business references for each executive officer. State the present salaries and/or other remunerations.

3. If a restricted stock option plan is in effect or is contemplated, deliver a copy of such a plan or an outline of the proposed plan, along with a schedule of options granted or to be granted, exercise prices, and grantees.

4. Include a statistical table showing for the last five years, if applicable, the number of employees at year-end and the total payroll expense. If profit-sharing or bonus plans were in effect for this period or any portion thereof, show such payments or appropriations in separate columns.

5. Include a statistical table that shows the departmental breakdown of the work force at the most recent date available. Show a further breakdown for the research department, if any, between engineers and nonengineers.

C. Business

1. Prepare a narrative description of historical development of the business, including the dates of any significant changes, such as acquisitions, introduction of new products, etc.

2. Describe the present product lines, providing as full a quantitative analysis as possible of the relative importance of each.

If possible, provide a sales analysis for the past several years. Provide an evaluation of each product with respect to quality, performance, etc., in comparison with competitors' products. Identify competitors in each line of products and compare percent of market possessed by subject company's product(s) with percentage possessed by the products of competitors in each product line. Describe in what ways the subject company believes its products have special competitive advantages over those of other producers.

3. Where products are of a technical nature, describe briefly the uses to which each principal product is put.

4. Describe marketing methods, including any significant changes in methods introduced in the last five years and the reasons for them. Provide a list of principal distributors, dealers, manufacturers' representatives, foreign agents, etc.

5. Identify and describe any patents believed to be of value to the subject; give expiration dates.

6. Provide an analysis of 20 principal customers in each of the last five years, giving annual dollar sales made to each. Describe any special agreements with any such customers. Give briefly the background facts explaining any relatively sharp gain or decline in sales to each of such customers in the last five years.

7. With respect to proprietary items, describe pricing policies on each important product line, including the current prices to distributors and distributors' prices to ultimate consumers or users. Compare subject company's prices with those of the principal competitors.

8. Describe as concretely as possible management planning in regard to product and market development over the next five years.

D. Industry

1. Where possible, give a statistical record of the industry or sub-industry in which the subject operates; indicate the sources of such statistical data.

2. Evaluate future prospects for the industry or sub-industry of the subject company. Any judgments should be supported by logical reasoning which leads to the conclusion.

3. Describe any technological trends or potentialities in or out of the subject company's industry that might materially and/or adversely affect the subject company's business.

E. Financial Statements and Operating Statistics

1. Furnish annual audited statements for the last five years. If audits are short forms only (i.e., no supporting schedules for major balance sheet items, cost of sales, and expense categories), also furnish internal fiscal year-end reports.

2. Furnish the most recent interim financial statements (need not be audited) in comparative form.

3. If the financial statements contain items or involve methods of treatment peculiar to industry or to the subject company, describe them.

4. Where applicable, furnish historical operating statistics as to unit sales, average realized prices, costs per unit, etc.

F. Financing Sought

1. Describe as specifically as possible the financing sought, including the amount, suggested form, and other concurrent financing if this is part of a larger plan.

2. As concretely as possible, describe the application of financing. If funds are to be used in whole or in part for construction or capital additions, provide detailed estimates of the cost of the program.

3. Furnish independent engineering reports, if any, which have been prepared in connection with the contemplated financing or business program.

4. If financing is in whole or in part for the purpose of buying out in whole or in part the subject company's stockholders, give details as to the individuals desiring to divest themselves of their holdings.

5. Estimate as concretely as possible the incremental earning power to be generated by the application of financing proceeds.

6. If further financing requirements are anticipated for the purpose of carrying out the subject company's future program, state the amount, timing, and management's thinking as to the form of the financial arrangements.

7. Furnish a balance sheet showing the projected effects of the financing that is presently sought.

8. Furnish cash flow and/or profit and loss forecasts covering the 24 months succeeding this financing. Describe all pertinent reasoning that supports such forecasts.

MARKET DEVELOPMENT CHECKLIST

William E. Hill and Co., Inc., a subsidiary of Dun and Bradstreet, Inc., has put together a checklist utilized for developing a marketing program.

A. Planning Stage

1. Identify and Measure Market Segments.
   a. Identify total market, including size and growth.
   b. Break market down into meaningful "business" segments, again including size and growth.
   c. Identify (typical) customers in each segment.
   d. Identify (typical) competitors in each segment, including profit and growth records of competitor.

2. Identify Market Characteristics for Each Segment (through Field Research)
   a. Identify end-user functional requirements (e.g., prestige, appeal).
   b. Identify end-user product requirements (types, extent of line, prices, quality, packaging service, product service, warranties, etc.).
   c. Determine end-user buying practices.
   d. Determine competitor marketing practices.

3. Determine Major Requirements for Success in Each Segment.
    a. Determine concept of the business or basic business policies.
    b. Determine product line.
    c. Plan marketing.
    d. Plan operations or production.
    e. Plan engineering, research, and new product development.

4. Project the Business and Our Company Profit Potential.
    a. Project growth forces in the market (or lack of same).
    b. Project technical trends (including product/process obsolescence).
    c. Project competitive trends (including capacity, vertical/ horizontal integration).
    d. Project market trends (including approaching saturation, population shifts, changes in merchandising, changes in buying habits).
    e. Make market and industry projections (physical units and dollar volume).
    f. Make projection of pricing climate (factors causing improvement or decline).
    g. Make projection of "our share" of market attainable.
    h. Project costs, investment, return on investment (five-year pro forma financial statements).

5. Develop Marketing Objective and Strategies.
    a. Evaluate company objectives vs. profit opportunities, company skills and resources, and company needs.
    b. Develop marketing objectives and strategies for each market segment.

B. Execution Stage

1. Determine Sales Force Requirements.
    a. Established customers: Determine requirements in regard to frequency and types of calls, persuasive selling, engineering selling, personal selling, executive selling, technical service, etc.
    b. Potential customers: Identify prime and secondary potential customers and their needs; determine requirements

in regard to frequency and type of primary sales contacts; bird dogging.

2. Determine Sales Administration to Facilitate Above Functions.

a. Decide upon a policy for determining sales "territories" and for distributing salesmen's accounts.
b. Develop sales organization and management.
c. Plan method for sales compensation and for review of salesmen's performance, quotas, or other standards; customer contact.
d. Plan methods of stimulating salesmen.

3. Determine Requirements for Service to Fill Customer Needs.

a. Plan for price and delivery quotations, order processing, scheduling and expediting of deliveries, and order follow-up.
b. Plan for technical service of product, if necessary.
c. Plan for shipping and physical distribution.
d. Plan for distributing sales correspondence, product information, and advertising literature.

4. Determine Advertising and Sales Promotion Requirements.

a. Advertising must reach both present and potential customers.

5. Determine Marketing Administration to Facilitate Above Functions.

a. Market research determines market trends and forecasting, makes sales analyses, identifies prime prospects, analyzes competitors, and obtains trade intelligence.
b. The marketing administration must work in conjunction with the developers of new products so that the new products can be marketed effectively.
c. Plan for advertising and sales promotion.
d. Positive pricing administration.
e. Select distributors and/or dealers carefully.
f. Recruit adequate personnel, then train them well, compensate them adequately, and frequently review their performance.
g. Plan marketing budgets, cost controls, and inventory control.
h. Plan to take care of both credits and collections.

i. Evaluate trade association affiliations.

j. Determine whether or not product or market managers can act as specialized assistants in marketing administration.

k. Plan for the handling of national or multi-salesman accounts.

l. Plan the total organization structure of marketing activities.

MARKETING FUNCTIONS CHECKLIST

William E. Hill and Co., Inc. has also assembled this marketing functions checklist.

A. Sales Operations
     Customer maintenance
          Periodic follow-up
          Engineering selling
          Personal selling
          Executive selling
          Service selling
     New customer development
     Bird dogging
     Customer service
     Intelligence feedback

B. Marketing Research and Planning
     Sales analysis by product
     Market share analysis
     Territory analysis
     Distribution analysis
     Account profitability analysis
     Market measurement
     Market forecasts
     Market characteristics
     Identification and classification of potential accounts
     New products research
     Test marketing
     Product planning
     Package planning
     "Long-range" planning
     Competitive, technical, and market trends
     Market intelligence center

C. Sales Management
     Sales organization
     Territories
     Use of accountants or other specialists
     Quotas and other performance standards
     Performance review
     Salesman stimulation
     Time and expense controls
     Call reports
     Compensation review

D. Advertising and Sales Promotion
     Advertising
          Creative development
          Media selection
          Sales coordination
     Sales promotion
          Salesman aids

Merchandise displays
Trade promotion
  literature
Public relations

E. Customer Service
Quotation and estimating
Order processing
Scheduling
Expediting and delivery
Specials
Technical service
Sales correspondence
Warranties
Adjustments

F. Physical Distribution
Warehousing
Shipping
Repackaging
Inventory control

G. Marketing Management
Marketing objectives
Market segments to pursue
Volume and profit goals

Overall marketing concept
Marketing strategy selection
Sales policies
Pricing policies
Policies in other areas
Credit, allowances
Budget and cost controls
Inventory control
Trade association member-
  ship
New product marketing-
  customer liaison
Use of product and/or
  market specialists
Key account aid
Overall marketing
  organization

H. Marketing Personnel
Selection
Recruitment
Training
Personnel records
Manpower planning

NOTES

[1]Donald M. Dible, *Up Your Own Organization*, The Entrepreneur Press, 1973, pages 331–352.

INDEX